Teaching to the Math Common Core State ...

Teaching to the Math Common Core State Standards

Focus on Kindergarten to Grade 5

F. D. Rivera
Department of Mathematics and Statistics
San Jose State University, California, USA

SENSE PUBLISHERS
ROTTERDAM/BOSTON/TAIPEI

A C.I.P. record for this book is available from the Library of Congress.

ISBN: 978-94-6209-501-4 (paperback)
ISBN: 978-94-6209-502-1 (hardback)
ISBN: 978-94-6209-503-8 (e-book)

Published by: Sense Publishers
P.O. Box 21858
3001 AW Rotterdam
The Netherlands
https://www.sensepublishers.com/

Printed on acid-free paper

CONTENTS

DEAR ELEMENTARY MAJORS AND PRACTICING AND BEGINNING ELEMENTARY TEACHERS: AN INTRODUCTION

This methods book takes a very practical approach to learning to teach elementary school mathematics in an emerging Age of the Common Core State Standards (CCSS). The Kindergarten through Grade 12 CCSS in Mathematics (i.e., CCSSM) was officially released on June 2, 2010 with 45 of the 50 US states in agreement to adopt it. Consequently, that action also meant implementing changes in their respective state standards and curriculum in mathematics. The CCSSM is not meant to be "the" official mathematics curriculum; it was purposefully developed primarily to provide clear learning expectations of mathematics content that are appropriate at every grade level and to help prepare all students to be ready for college and the workplace. A quick glance at the Table of Contents in this book indicates a serious engagement with the recommended mathematics underlying the kindergarten through grade 5 portions of the CCSSM first, with issues in assessment, learning, teaching, and classroom management pursued next and in that order.

One implication of the CCSSM for you who are in the process of learning to teach the subject involves understanding shared explicit content and practice standards in the teaching, learning, and assessment of elementary school mathematics. The content standards, which pertain to mathematical knowledge, skills, and applications, have been carefully crafted so that they are "teachable and learnable," that is, smaller than typical in scope, coherent, inch-deep versus mile-wide, focused, and rigorous. According to the Gates Foundation that initially supported the development of the CCSSM, "(t)he new mathematics ... standards were built to be teachable and concrete—there are fewer, and they are clearer. And the standards were built on the evidence of what is required for success beyond high school—these standards aim higher." Further, "coherent" in the CCSSM means to say that the content standards "convey a unified vision of the big ideas and supporting concepts ... and reflect a progression of learning that is meaningful and appropriate." The practice standards, which refer to institutionally valued mathematical actions, processes, and habits, have been conceptualized in ways that will hopefully encourage all elementary students to engage with the content standards more deeply than merely acquiring mathematical knowledge by rote and imitation. An instance of this content-practice relationship involves patterns in arithmetic. When elementary students are asked to develop valid algorithms for combining whole numbers (i.e., operations), they

1

should also be provided with an opportunity to engage in mathematical practices such as looking for structures and expressing the regularity of such structures in repeated reasoning.

So, unlike "typical" state standards that basically provide (sound) outlines of mathematical content in different ways, the CCSSM puts premium on this content-practice nexus, with instruction orchestrating purposeful experiences that enable all students to develop the expert habits of mathematicians and to struggle productively as they grow in mathematical maturity and competence. To perceive the CCSSM merely in terms of redistributing mathematics content that works for all 45 states defeats the purpose in which it was formulated in the first place. That is, the CCSSM is not about covering either the content or practice of school mathematics; it is un/covering content-practices that can support meaningful mathematical acquisition and understanding of concepts, skills, and applications in order to encourage all elementary students to see value in the subject, succeed, progress toward middle school, and be prepared for careers that require 21st century skills.

One important consequence of this reconceptualized content-practice approach to learning elementary school mathematics involves making changes in the way students are assessed for mathematical proficiency. Typical content-driven state assessments would have, say, second- or third-grade students bubbling in a single correct answer in a multiple-choice item, for instance, choosing the largest value from several choices of four unit fractions. A CCSSM-driven assessment would have them justifying conditions that make such comparisons possible and valid from a mathematical point of view. Thus, in the CCSSM, proficiency in content alone is not sufficient, and so does practice without content, which is limited. Content and practice are both equally important and, thus, must come together in teaching, learning, and assessment in order to support growth in students' mathematical understanding. "One hallmark of mathematical understanding," as noted in the CCSSM,

> is the ability to justify, in a way appropriate to the student's mathematical maturity, why a particular mathematical statement is true or where a mathematical rule comes from. There is a world of difference between a student who can summon a mnemonic device ... and a student who can explain where the mnemonic comes from. The student who can explain the rule understands the mathematics, and may have a better chance to succeed at a less familiar task .... Mathematical understanding and procedural skill are equally important, and both are assessable using mathematical tasks of sufficient richness.

As a document that has been adopted for use in 45 US states, the CCSSM developed appropriate content standards - mathematical knowledge, skills, and applications – at each grade level that all students need to know regardless of their location and context. Such standards are not to be viewed merely as a list of competencies. As noted earlier, which is worth reemphasizing, they have been drawn from documented research on learning paths that students tend to pursue, from the initial and informal phase of sense making and adaptive thinking to the more formal and sophisticated phase of necessary mathematical knowledge. Implications of various learning paths then became the basis for designing coherent progressions of mathematical concepts and processes from one grade level to the next. It is this particular constraint that should remind you that you are teaching *not* to the common core of mathematics but to the CCSSM. Certainly, there are other possible learning paths in, say, understanding whole numbers and fractions, which should be encouraged and supported. But you must persevere to care and to see to it that the way you teach elementary mathematics is supportive of the intentions of the CCSSM.

The CCSSM content standards have also been informed by the best available evidence from research and practices across states. Further, they reflect in sufficient terms the content standards of the highest-performing countries in mathematics. Consequently, you will enter the teaching profession with this available knowledge base that you are expected to know really well and should be able to teach. Certainly, there is always room for interpretation, innovation, and creativity, especially in the implementation phase. However, the CCSSM is unequivocal about the consistent learning expectations of mathematical competence at every grade level, so fidelity is crucial at this early stage in the CCSSM implementation. Own it since you are its very first users. Test it to so that it makes a difference and produces a long-term positive impact on your students. Both the National Governors Association and the Council of Chief State School Officers that sponsored the CCSSM initiative point out that the CCSSM "standards are a common sense first step toward ensuring our children are getting the best possible education no what where they live" and "give educators shared goals and expectations for their students." And a much greater focus on fewer topics based on coherent learning progressions should make the content-practice doable in every math class. Hence, under the CCSSM framework, you no longer pick and choose content. Instead, you teach for content-practice expertise.

With clear content-practice standards in the CCSSM, a common comprehensive assessment also became a necessity. As the Gordon Commission have pointed out in relation to the future of education, the troika of assessment, teaching, and learning forms the backbone of a well-conceptualized pedagogy. While the three processes can take place independently, they should co-exist in a mutually determining context. Hence, for you, it means developing a mindset of alignment. In actual practice, in fact, it is impossible in school contexts to conceptualize teaching that has not been informed by any form of assessment of student learning. Further, the basic aim of assessment and teaching is improved learning, no less. Given this mindset of alignment, the *Smarter Balanced Assessment* (SBA) and the *Partnership for Assessment of Readiness for College and Careers* (PARCC) emerged, two independent consortia of states that agreed to develop "next-generation assessments" that are aligned with the CCSSM and ready to be implemented by the 2014-2015 school year. At the core of such high-stakes assessments involves measuring student progress and pathways toward college and college readiness. For you, this institutional expectation of assessment practice also means understanding what is at stake and what is needed to help your students succeed in such high-quality assessments.

Suffice it to say, the realities of the CCSSM, SBA, and PARCC in schools will drive issues of learning, teaching, assessment, and classroom management, including your choice of professional growth and development. Any responsible and thoughtful professional can cope with and work within and around such constraints, and this methods book intends to provide you with support that will help you begin to teach to the CCSSM. In past practices, a typical elementary methods course in mathematics would begin with general and domain-specific issues in learning and teaching with content knowledge emerging in the process. The approach that is used in this particular book assumes the opposite view by situating reflections and issues in learning and teaching elementary school mathematics around constraints in content-practice standards and assessment. Like any profession that involves some level of accountability, the manner in which you are expected to teach mathematics in today's times has to embrace such realities, which also means needing to arm yourself with a proactive disposition that will support all elementary students succeed in developing mathematical understanding necessary for middle school and beyond, including the workplace. It is worth noting that the development of the CCSSM, SBA, and PARCC, everything else having been considered, relied heavily on perspectives from various stakeholders such as teachers, school administrators, state leaders and policymakers, experts, educators, researchers, and parents and community groups. For you, this particular collaborative context of the CCSSM, SBA, and PARCC means understanding and appreciating both the efforts and the framing contexts of their emergence. It takes a village for these state-driven initiatives to succeed, and it is now your turn to be in the front line of change.

1.1 A BLENDED MULTISOURCED APPROACH TO LEARNING TO TEACH MATHEMATICS

Considering the vast amount of information that is readily available on the internet, including your digital-native disposition and competence toward conducting online searches of various kinds of information, this book explores the possibility of a blended multisourced approach to methods of teaching elementary school mathematics. Embedded in several sections of this book are activities that will require you to access online information. Becoming acquainted and getting used to this blended form of learning, as a matter of fact, provide good training for the actual work that comes. That is, once you start teaching, you no longer have to plan alone. You do not have to wait for a face-to-face professional development workshop to learn new ideas. You can gain access to resources with very minimal cost, and in many cases at no cost to you. What is always needed, however, which applies to any kind of profession, is some kind of training that involves knowing where and how to look for correct and appropriate information. Many sections in this book will require you to access links that provide the best information. From a practice standpoint, the blended multisourced approach taken in this book symbolizes the collaborative nature of preparing to teach, which you know and which seasoned teachers should affirm depend on a repertoire of tools that you gain by learning from other sources.

For convenience, you are strongly encouraged to access the following free site below, which contains all the links, articles, and reproducible worksheets in a document format that are referenced in various sections in this book. The site was informed and is respectful of copyright rules, so exercise care on matters involving dissemination.

http://commoncoreelementarymethods.wikispaces.com/

1.2 OVERVIEW OF THE REMAINING CHAPTERS

Chapter 2 introduces you to the eight CCSSM practice standards. Content activities are provided to help you understand the content-practice dimension of teaching, learning, and assessing school mathematics. You will also learn in some detail important psychological and instructional issues surrounding problem solving, reasoning and proof, representations, communications, and connections. Take a peek at Figure 2.1 (p. 12) for an interpretive visual summary of the eight practice standards. Content-practice teaching, learning, and assessment together involves mapping mathematical content and appropriate practices in the development and emergence of (school) mathematical knowledge.

Chapters 3 through 9 deal with content-practice, teaching, and learning issues relevant to the following six domains below that comprise the kindergarten through grade 5 CCSSM.

– Counting and cardinality (*Chapter 3*)
– Whole numbers and operations in base 10 (*Chapters 4 and 6*)
– Operations and algebraic thinking (*Chapter 5*)
– Fractions and operations (*Chapter 7*)
– Geometry (*Chapter 8*)
– Measurement and data (*Chapter 9*)

Domains consist of clusters or organized groups of related content standards, where each standard defines in explicit terms what students need to understand and be able to do. By the end of fifth grade CCSSM, all students should have a firm grasp of the power-of-10 place value structure of whole numbers and decimals up to the hundredths place, including operations and applications. They should also be able to perform addition, subtraction, and multiplication of fractions with like and unlike denominators. Fraction division knowledge does not include the case where both the numerator and denominator are fractions, which they pursue in sixth grade. In geometry, their content knowledge of polygons and circles closes with classifications of parallelograms and the rectangular coordinate system, where points as locations in space are described as ordered pairs of numbers. They learn about ordered pairs and the rectangular coordinate system when they explore multiple representations of linear patterns. In measurement, they consistently employ a multiplicative approach

5

when they learn to tell time, obtain totals and other results involving money, and measure and convert in exact terms lengths of segments, areas of closed polygonal figures, volumes of 3D shapes, and angles. In data, they deal with contexts involving discrete variables. They learn to represent them graphically in different ways and especially with line plots, which are emphasized from second through fifth grade. Overall, the numbers that matter from kindergarten to grade 5 are whole numbers, decimal numbers up to the hundredths, and fractions. Negative numbers are formally introduced in the sixth grade CCSSM in the context of system of rational numbers. Variables are also formally introduced in sixth grade CCSSM in the context of expressions and equations.

Chapter 10 addresses different assessment strategies that measure elementary students' understanding of the CCSSM. It also introduces you to the basic structure and testing requirements of the SBA. You will learn about formative and summative assessments and norm- and criterion-referenced testing, including alternative forms of assessment such as journal writing and unit projects as extended versions of a SBA performance task. Sections that deal with the SBA can be replaced by or discussed together with PARCC, if you find it necessary to do so. In the closing section, you will develop content-practice assessment tasks for practice.

Chapter 11 relies on information drawn from the preceding chapters. You will deal with issues that are relevant to elementary students' learning of mathematics within the constraints of the CCSSM and SBA (or PARCC). The complex historical relationship between learning theories and the US school mathematics curriculum throughout the years, including the *Math Wars*, are also discussed in order to help you understand the negative consequences of holding extreme views on mathematical learning. Further, you will explore in some detail the theories of Piaget and Vygotsky with the intent of helping you understand Fuson's integrated learning-path developmentally appropriate learning/teaching model, which emphasizes growth in elementary students' understanding and fluency of mathematics. Fuson's model offers a middle ground that opposes extreme views and corrects various misreadings of constructivist and sociocultural learning in mathematical contexts.

Chapter 12 addresses practical issues relevant to teaching the CCSSM in elementary school classrooms. You will learn different teaching models and write content-practice unit, lesson, and assessment plans.

Chapter 13 focuses on issues relevant to setting up and running an effective mathematics classroom that is conducive for teaching and learning the CCSSM. You will become familiar with issues surrounding student persistence and motivation in mathematics, including ways that can help you design learning and learning environments that foster flexible problem solving and mathematical disposition. You will also be introduced to Complex Instruction, an equity-driven approach to group or collaborative learning in the mathematics classroom. General classroom management concerns close the chapter, which deal with how to design and manage optimal learning for all students, eliminate or minimize disruptions, and address potential behavior problems.

GETTING TO KNOW THE COMMON CORE STATE STANDARDS FOR MATHEMATICAL PRACTICE

This chapter introduces you to the eight Common Core State Standards for Mathematical Practice (CCSSMP; "practice standards"). Take a moment to access the information from the following link: http://www.corestandards.org/Math/Practice.

The practice standards explicitly articulate how elementary students should engage with the Common Core State Standards for mathematical content (or "content standards") "as they grow in mathematical maturity and expertise throughout the [elementary] years" (NGACBP &CCSSO, 2012, p. 8). That is, when you teach to the content standards, the practice standards should help inform and guide how you teach, how your students develop mathematical understanding, and what and how you assess for content knowledge. Consistent with the overall intent of the Common Core State Standards in Mathematics (CCSSM), the content and practice standards convey shared goals and expectations about the kinds of knowledge, skills, applications, and proficiencies that will help all elementary students succeed in mathematics and be ready for workplace demands. The practice standards appear to be relevant to other subjects as well, making them powerful, interesting, and useful to elementary students who are in the process of learning to systematically make sense of different objects and relationships in terms of structures. Structures yield patterns as a consequence of explicit and well-defined rules that characterize them and make reasoning possible.

As you pay attention to content-practice relationships in this chapter, do not lose sight of the assessment aspect of learning, which you will pursue in some detail in Chapter 10 in connection with the Smarter Balanced Assessment. Even if this chapter focuses on the learning and teaching of a few topics in elementary school mathematics in order to demonstrate ways in which mathematical practices support content learning, it is good to have an *alignment mindset* at all times. Always remind yourself that effective and meaningful pedagogy is a fundamental matter of alignment among mathematics curriculum, learning, teaching, and assessment.

2.1 CONTENT ACTIVITY 1: GENERATING ADDITION FACTS

Think about how kindergarten (K) students may be taught to decompose whole numbers that are less than or equal to 10 into pairs in several different ways (e.g., $4 = 2 + 2$ and $4 = 1 + 3$; **K.OA.A.3**). When you have an opportunity to work with them, you may want to provide them with concrete objects to work with such as two petri dishes (or any pair of small open containers), circle chips, plastic jelly beans, pattern blocks,unifix cubes, or unit cubes that will enable them to distribute objects into two sets. Or, encourage them to use their two hands to help them make sense of the decomposition activity. When they are ready, use Activity Sheet 2.1 or something similar to help them record all their decompositions in paper. If they can easily write numbers, ask them to translate what they draw in numerical form. In your case, work with a pair and use the structure of Activity Sheet 2.1 to help you generate all addition pairs for the whole number 10. See to it that you take turns in providing a response. Activity 2.1 shows an example involving the whole number 6, an appropriate size for K students. When you have completed the activity, discuss the following questions below with your pair.

a. Does your work show a systematic way of generating all the pairs for the number 10? If your work does not exhibit some systematic approach to the task, try to establish one.

My Addition Pairs for the Number 6	
How I See My Pairs	How I Want Adults to See My Pairs

Activity Sheet 2.1. Addition fact sheet

b. What might it mean for your work to be systematic? What might it mean for solutions to be systematic in a mathematical sense?

c. Do children and adults share the same understanding of systematic work in school mathematics? How about adults and mathematicians? Why or why not?

d. K students can use concrete object to help them count and accomplish the decomposition task. They can also use their hands to do the same task. Discuss advantages and disadvantages of each tool.

Basic addition number pairs or addition facts at the K level involve combinations of 1-digit numbers, also called *addends*, that are connected by the addition operation. All the addition facts should be automatic to you as an adult learner, which means that you do not need extra effort to generate them because you know what they are without having to either draw them or rely on manipulatives. That expertise is what you need to teach to K students. But as a teacher you also need to know how K students can be taught to be systematic so that they simply do not generate pairs by accident. From a mathematical point of view, you need to pay attention to at least three things. First, how might you generate all pairs systematically? Second, how do you know that you have all the required pairs for a given whole number? Third, what mathematical practices do you want K students to learn from accomplishing the task?

Consider the following systematic way of generating number pairs using your two hands. Focus on the whole number 5. Show 5 with your left hand. Notice that you used all five fingers on your left hand and no finger on your right hand. In a numerical format, you can record that as $5 = 5 + 0$, your starting addition pair.

From the starting pair, take away 1 finger on the left hand and raise 1 finger on the right hand. Verify that it shows $5 = 4 + 1$, your second addition pair. This simultaneous process of subtracting-and-adding 1 is often referred to as an *additive compensation* strategy. In general, additive compensation is a give-and-take away strategy, which involves adding a number to one addend and subtracting the same number from the other addend.

From the second addition pair, apply compensation once again by taking away 1 finger on the left hand and raising another finger on the right hand. What third addition pair is evident from your action?

Keep doing the same action until you have exhausted all the fingers on your left hand. Verify the following addition facts for 5 below.

$$5 = 5 + 0$$
$$5 = 4 + 1$$
$$5 = 3 + 2$$
$$5 = 2 + 3$$
$$5 = 1 + 4$$
$$5 = 0 + 5$$

When you work with K students, the above list can help them begin to investigate the arithmetical property of *commutativity* involving addition. The commutative property for addition states that when you add a pair of addends, the order in which you add them does not and should not affect the result of addition called *sum*. When children see six different addition number facts for the whole number 5, you may draw on their physical experiences with their pairs of hands to help them understand why there should only be three distinct number facts for the whole number 5. You may also use the same occasion to ask them whether it is possible to generate more than three distinct number pairs for 5.

Repeat the same sequence of actions above to generate all distinct addition facts for whole numbers from 0 to 10. Use Activity Sheet 2.2 to record your answers and respond to the questions below.

e. Explain the significance of the commutative property for addition in the number-pair activity.

f. What benefits do K students gain from learning additive compensation early in their mathematical experiences? What issues (cognitive, developmental, linguistic, etc.) might they have in learning to apply additive compensation, and how might you help them overcome those issues?

g. What benefits do K students gain from repeating the same sequence of actions over several instances of whole numbers?

Number Pairs for 0	Number Pairs for 1	Number Pairs for 2	Number Pairs for 3	Number Pairs for 4
Number Pairs for 6	Number Pairs for 7	Number Pairs for 8	Number Pairs for 9	Number Pairs for 10

Activity Sheet 2.2. Paired decompositions for whole numbers up to 10

h. Using one's pair of hands is a good way of learning how to benchmark by 5. How might that be accomplished? What potential difficulties might K students experience with that strategy?

i. Explain how you might use additive compensation to generate all distinct addition facts for whole numbers greater than 10.

j. Some teachers use story problems as a way of contextualizing this particular number pair activity. Search the internet for examples of such problems and then discuss advantages and potential issues.

k. Establish a general strategy that will help you obtain all distinct addition triples (i.e., 3 addends) for any whole number. Think of *general strategy* in terms of a *rule* that works all the time within the cases being considered (also called *domain*).

2.2 THE EIGHT COMMON CORE STATE STANDARDS FOR MATHEMATICAL PRACTICE

Figure 2.1 shows an interpretive visual model of the CCSSM practice standards. The standards have been derived from two important documents that describe processes and proficiencies that are central to the learning of school mathematics. The National Council of Teachers of Mathematics (NCTM) identifies problem solving, reasoning and proof, communication, representation, and connections to be the most significant processes that all elementary students should learn well. The National Research Council (NRC) characterizes mathematically proficient students in terms of their mathematical competence in the strands of adaptive reasoning, strategic competence, conceptual understanding, procedural fluency, and productive disposition. Tables 2.1 and 2.2 list the characteristics of the NCTM process standards and the NRC proficiency strands, respectively. Read them carefully and highlight terms and descriptions that you think would need some clarification.

To better appreciate the CCSSM practice standards, explore the following mathematical task, *Building a Hexagon Flower Garden Design,* from the points of view of the NCTM process standards and the NRC proficiency strands. The task involves generating and analyzing an emerging pattern, which is an appropriate problem solving activity for fifth grade students (**5.OA.3**).

2.3 CONTENT ACTIVITY 2: BUILDING A HEXAGON FLOWER GARDEN DESIGN

Figure 2.2 shows a hexagon flower garden design of size 4 that will be used to cover a flat horizontal walkway between two rooms. A design of size 1 consists of a black hexagon tile that is surrounded by six gray hexagon tiles.

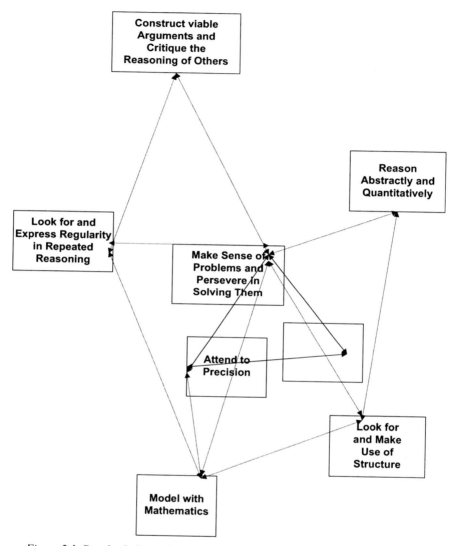

Figure 2.1. Standards for mathematical practice. (NGACBP & CCSSO, 2012, pp. 6-8)

Table 2.1. The NCTM Process Standards (NCTM, 2000)

Problem Solving (PS)	Reasoning and Proof (RP)
1. build new mathematical knowledge through problem solving;	1. recognize reasoning and proof as fundamental aspects of mathematics;
2. solve problems that arise in mathematics and in other contexts;	2. make and investigate mathematical conjectures;
3. apply and adapt a variety of appropriate strategies to solve problems;	3. develop and evaluate mathematical arguments and proofs;
4. monitor and reflect on the process of mathematical problem solving.	4. select and use various types of reasoning and methods of proof.
Communication (CM)	Connections (CN)
1. organize and consolidate their mathematical thinking through communication;	1. recognize and use connections among mathematical ideas;
2. communicate their mathematical thinking coherently and clearly to peers, teachers, and others;	2. understand how mathematical ideas interconnect and build on one another to produce a coherent whole;
3. analyze and evaluate the mathematical thinking and strategies of others;	3. recognize and apply mathematics in contexts outside of mathematics.
4. use the language of mathematics to express mathematical ideas precisely.	

Representation (RP)
1. create and use representations to organize, record, and communicate mathematical ideas;
2. select, apply, and translate among mathematical representations to solve problems;
3. use representations to model and interpret physical, social, and mathematical phenomena.

Table 2.2. The NRC Mathematical Proficiency Strands (NRC, 2001)

Conceptual Understanding (CU)	Procedural Fluency (PF)
comprehension of mathematical concepts, operations, and relations	skill in carrying out procedures flexibly, accurately, efficiently, and appropriately
Strategic Competence (SC)	Adaptive Reasoning (AR)
ability to formulate, represent, and solve mathematical problems	capacity for logical thought, reflection, explanation, and justification

Productive Disposition (PD)
habitual inclination to see mathematics as sensible, useful, worthwhile, coupled with a belief in diligence and one's own efficacy

Figure 2.2. Hexagon flower garden path of size 4

a. Figure 2.2 is a garden design of size 4. How many black and gray hexagon tiles are there?

b. Work with a pair and complete Activity Sheet 2.3 together. What do the four equal signs (=) mean in the context of the activity?

c. Many expert patterners will most likely infer that on the basis of the assumptions stated for the problem and the data collected in Activity Sheet 2.3 the mathematical relationship appears to model a specific rule. Think of "inference" as "going beyond the data." What information relevant to the task and the limited data shown in Activity 2.3 will help them establish that inference?

d. On the basis of the assumptions noted in (c), three Grade 5 students identified the following features of the pattern below relative to the number of gray hexagon tiles for a design of size 12.

Ava: Keep adding 4, so 2, 2 + 4 = 6, 6 + 4 = 10, 10 + 4 = 14, ..., 46 + 4 = 50.

Bert: Add 12 groups of 4 brown tiles and then add 2 more. It's like the times table for 4. So, 4, 8, 12, ..., 40, 44, 48. Then plus 2 you get 50.

Ces: Double 12 groups of 2 brown tiles. Then add 2 more. It's like the times table for 2 plus 1. So 2, 4, 6, 8, ..., 20, 22, 24, 25. Then you double it and you get 50.

Which student is correct, and why? How does each student see his or her pattern relative to the size-12 design?

It seems that Bert and Ces are comparing two sequences of numbers. For Bert his terms in the new sequence are 2 more than 4 times the corresponding terms in a familiar sequence. For Ces her terms in the new sequence are 1 more than twice the corresponding terms in a familiar sequence that she then double in value. Do their rules make sense? Explain.

e. Ava gives Bert 75 brown hexagon tiles in groups of 10. As soon as Bert receives the last tile, he tells her, "It's odd, so I really can't use all the tiles. Do you want 1 tile back?" Ava thinks Bert is not correct. What do you think? If Bert is correct, how does he know so quickly?

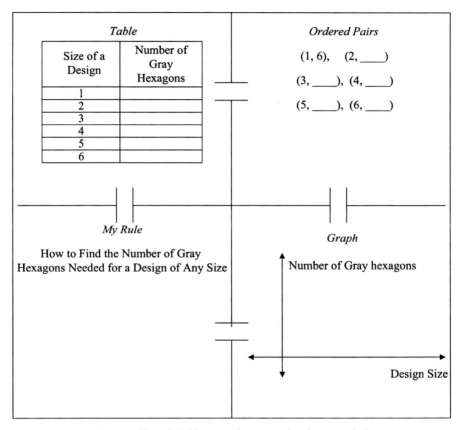

Activity Sheet 2.3. Hexagon flower garden design task data

Consider your mathematical experience with the *Building a Hexagon Flower Garden Design* task. Work in groups of 3 and discuss the following questions below. For each group, assign a facilitator, a recorder or scribe, and a reporter. The facilitator needs to make sure that all members of the group are able to share their experiences. The recorder or scribe should see to it that the group report reflects contributions from all members of your group. The reporter is responsible for sharing your group's views in the follow up whole-classroom discussion. Exercise care and caution as you perform your respective roles so that you all feel respected and are able to make significant contributions in the process of working together.

f. Refer to Table 2.1. To what extent did the patterning task encourage you to engage in:
   i. at least one of four problem solving actions?
   ii. at least one of four reasoning and proof actions?

    iii. at least one of four communication actions?
    iv. at least one of three connection actions?
    v. at least one of three representational actions?

g. Refer to Table 2.2. This time keep in mind the needs of Grade 5 students.
    i. What mathematical concepts, operations, relations, and skills do they need in order to successfully construct and justify rules such as the ones that Bert and Ces produced in item (d)? In mathematics, such rules are called *direct expressions.*
    ii. How does having a deep understanding of relationships in a multiplication table help them construct direct expressions?
    ii. What purpose and value does item (d) serve in their developing understanding of patterns?
    iv. How do patterning tasks help them develop productive disposition?

In the next succeeding five sections, you will explore the NCTM process standards in some detail, providing you with a better understanding of the issues underlying the practice standards and the work that is required to implement them effectively in your own classrooms.

2.4 PROBLEM SOLVING CONTEXTS IN ELEMENTARY SCHOOL MATHEMATICS

Problem solving contexts in elementary school mathematics are drawn from a variety of situations, as follows:

1. authentic and real situations, where mathematics emerges naturally in the context of everyday experiences;
2. conceptually real situations, where mathematics emerges from well-described scenarios that are difficult or almost impossible to be modeled in real time but nonetheless contain sufficient information that will help students perform the relevant actions mentally;
3. simulated (i.e., imitated) situations, where mathematics emerges from situations that are modeled in a technological platform because they: (i) are inaccessible at the physical level; (ii) cannot be accomplished in the classroom; or (iii) are meant to conveniently illustrate an instructional objective; and
4. context-free mathematical situations, where mathematics emerges from tasks that consist of symbols that students manipulate according to well defined rules or principles.

2.4.1 Content Activity 3: Different Types of Problems in Elementary School Mathematics

Access the following link, which will take you to the Smarter Balanced Assessment released mathematics sample items for Grades 3 to 5 students: http://sampleitems.

smarterbalanced.org/itempreview/sbac/index.htm. Work with a pair and answer the following questions below.

a. Solve each sample item first before moving on to the next two tasks below.
b. Draw on your experiences to help you classify each item according to the type of problem solving context it models.
c. Choose five of your favorite sample items. For each item, list the proficiencies that you think are appropriate for students to model and accomplish successfully. Your analysis do not have to reflect all five NRC proficiency strands.

2.5 REPRESENTATIONS IN ELEMENTARY SCHOOL MATHEMATICS

When you ask elementary school students to establish an external representation of a mathematical object, they need to find a way of portraying the object and capturing its essential attributes in some recognizable form. Representations range in type from personal to institutional, informal to formal, and approximate to exact depending on the context in which they arise in mathematical activity. Personal, informal, and approximate representations often reflect individual worldviews, so their forms tend to be idiosyncratic and situated (i.e., they make sense only to the individual). Institutional, formal, and exact representations involve the use of shared inscriptions, rules for combining them, and a well-defined and well-articulated system that links symbols and rules according to the requirements, practices, and traditions of institutions that support their emergence.

Meaningful representations at the elementary level develop in an emergent context beginning with what children know and how they convey them. There is no other way, in fact, and the goal of teaching involves finding ways that will effectively **bridge** the personal with the formal through negotiation either between you as the teacher and your students or among students in an engaging activity. Figure 2.3 visually captures the context emergence in terms of ongoing and often nonlinear progressions in representational competence.

2.5.1 Content Activity 4: A Kindergarten Subtraction Task

Consider the following K subtraction task below, which involves a take-away situation (**K.OA.1** and **K.OA.2**). Answer the questions that follow.
Marla has 10 pencils. She gives 4 pencils to her brother. How many pencils does she have left?

a. How might K students represent the above problem in the absence of formal instruction?
b. How might they be taught to solve the problem in the classroom without any formal instruction on place value representations of whole numbers?
c. How does a place-value solution help K students in the long term?

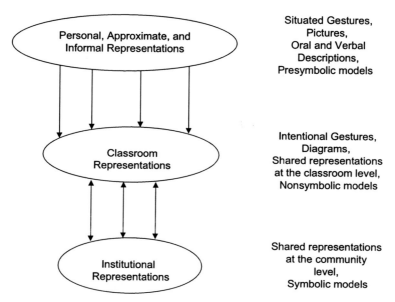

Situated Gestures,
Pictures,
Oral and Verbal
Descriptions,
Presymbolic models

Intentional Gestures,
Diagrams,
Shared representations
at the classroom level,
Nonsymbolic models

Shared representations
at the community
level,
Symbolic models

Figure 2.3. Progressive formalization and mathematization of representations

Personal, approximate, and informal representations involve the use of situated gestures, pictures, and verbal expressions. Some K students may solve the above take-away problem by using their fingers to count. Others may draw pictures of 10 pencils in which case you need to give them time to draw. In either case of representation, they are likely to engage in a counting all strategy. For example, a student might initially count all the way to 10 by putting up all her fingers ("1, 2, 3, ..., 8, 9, 10"). Then she might put down 4 fingers and then count the remaining fingers ("1, 2, 3, 4, 5, 6"). Also, depending on their language competence, the accompanying oral descriptions may be very detailed and sometimes loaded with irrelevant information. Overall, such representations convey *presymbolic* models that are situated (i.e., context-dependent) and may be unstructured (i.e., unorganized and naïve) or structured (i.e., sophisticated) in form. Such models are usually inductively inferred, which means that they reflect repeated actions on similar problems and nothing else beyond that. Students who manage to solve the subtraction task and other similar examples by relying on their fingers to count are still not thinking at the level of "subtraction rules" that apply to all problems of that type.

Classroom representations mark the beginning of progressive formalization. Students' gestures in this phase tend to be purposeful and intentional as a result of their intense and shared interactions with you and others learners. Diagrams and other placeholder visuals such as sticks or circles replace actions of counting with fingers or drawing detailed pictures of pencils. Depending on their counting competence, they may also be taught to either count up to 10 from 4 ("4 in my head, so 5, 6, 7, … 9, 10. There are 6 left.") or count down from 10 until 4 fingers or objects have been taken away ("10, 9, 8, 7, so there are 6 left"). Further, they may be capable of writing down or recording a number sentence on paper ("$10 - 4 = 6$.").

Classroom representations achieve their meaningful progressively formal state when elementary students begin to coordinate the following two *nonsymbolic* aspects of their representations below.

1. *Analytic Condition*: Knowing how to process problems deductively by applying the appropriate rules;
2. *Abstract Entity Condition*: Using formal symbols to translate problems in external form.

In this particular characterization of classroom representation, elementary students are capable of thinking in terms of rules. In the presymbolic phase, specific instances over rules dominate representational action. In the nonsymbolic phase, the reverse is evident. In the case of the subtraction task, for example, the numbers 10, 4, and 6 are classified as *arithmetical quantities,* that is, numerals with units. The number sentence,

$$10 - 4 = 6$$

actually means

$$10 \text{ pencils} - 4 \text{ pencils} = 6 \text{ pencils}.$$

Another interesting characteristic of classroom representations is the condensed or contracted nature of the forms involving alphanumeric expressions that replace the oral and verbal descriptions that are evident in the presymbolic phase.

Institutional representations convey formal and shared representations at the community level. Since school mathematics content reflects the values, traditions, and practices of the entire mathematics community, elementary school students need to acquire appropriate and intentional ways of representing objects and relationships in order to participate meaningfully in the larger community. Institutional representations evolve into *symbolic* models as soon as children begin to decontextualize the problems, that is, by shifting their attention from the contexts to the processing of entities.Think about the subtraction take-away task once again. Problems of that type evolve in purpose over time in the elementary school mathematics curriculum. In kindergarten, children process them using objects or drawings (**K.OA.2**). In first grade, they represent them using place value structures (**1.NBT.2**) and with larger numbers (**1.OA.1** and**1.OA.6**). In second and third grade, they deal with differences (i.e. the result of subtracting two whole numbers) that extend to 100 (**2.NBT.5**) and 1000 (**3.NBT.2**), respectively. In fourth grade, they subtract multidigit whole numbers using the standard algorithm (**4.NBT.4**).

Moving on to a different aspect of representation, some mathematical objects are known to generate *multiple representations*, that is, they can be expressed in several different ways. For example, Activity Sheet 2.3 illustrates four different ways of representing the same pattern. Do the following activity below and answer the questions that follow.

2.5.2 Content Activity 5: Representing Whole Numbers in Second Grade

A formal mathematical structure for understanding 2-, 3-, and multi-digit whole numbers begins in first grade, which involves place value (**1.NBT.2**). Several more concepts relevant to place value structures of whole numbers are introduced in second grade, which focuses on 3-digit whole numbers (**2.NBT.1** and **2.NBT.3**).

d. Carefully read standard **2.NBT.1** and **2.NBT.3**. There are three representations that second-grade students need to learn. Name a 3-digit whole number and represent it in three different ways.
e. Develop a graphic organizer for (d). For a model, refer to Activity Sheet 2.3.
f. Think about all mathematical objects that have multiple representations. Many elementary teachers tend to teach all the relevant representations involving the same object at the same time. Do you agree? Discuss advantages of, and possible concerns with, this particular practice.

2.6 CONNECTIONS IN ELEMENTARY SCHOOL MATHEMATICS

One important aspect of your job involves helping elementary students establish connections among mathematical ideas. If you think of connections in terms of *relations*, then mathematical ideas are in fact linked in at least two different ways depending on the context of activity, as follows:

- *Representational connections* involve matters that pertain to *equivalence*, which means that two or more representations convey the same idea despite the superficial appearance of looking different. Consider, for example, the multiple representations for the same pattern shown in Activity Sheet 2.3. The table, set of ordered pairs, graph, and rule are all equivalent representations of the same pattern shown in Figure 2.2. They also hold the same assumptions about the pattern, which further support their equivalence. Take note of the four equal symbols shown in Activity Sheet 2.3, which convey the sense that equal means "is the same as."
- *Topical connections* involve linking two or more separate topics either from the same subject (e.g., fundamental operations in arithmetic and algebra) or from different subjects (e.g., patterns in mathematics and patterns in weather in elementary science).

Meaningful connections should facilitate *transfer*, which is a core process that supports thinking and learning about structures. Transfer involves applying what one has learned in one situation to another situation. But that is usually easier said than done. Since transfer is a subjective experience for individual learners, meaning to say that they need to establish the connections or relationships between two or more situations, representations, or topics themselves. Certainly, the subjective process can be smoothly facilitated by providing them with tools at the appropriate time that will enable them to see those connections as similar in some way. In other words, connections among representations and topics do not transfer on their own. Learners need to construct them with appropriate resources at their disposal. Such resources can be concrete (e.g., using manipulatives) or interventional (e.g., using purposeful guide questions) to help them accomplish successful transfer. The following activity exemplifies topical connections. Work with a pair and answer the questions that follow.

2.6.1 Content Activity 6: Repeating Patterns

Young children find activities with repeating patterns easy and interesting. Such patterns appear as groups of entities (i.e., numbers, letters, pictures, etc.) that repeat over and over. Each group represents a well-defined *core* (also called *common unit*) and one repetition of a core is called a *cycle*. The repeating pattern below represents a string of geometric shapes that consists of three cycles. In the CCSSM, there is no mention of repeating patterns at all. However, they are worth exploring with K and first grade students because of their simple mathematical structure. Such structures often have well-defined rules that enable students to quickly infer whether an entity belongs to the pattern or does not belong to the pattern. Work with a pair and answer the questions below.

Shape	○	△	□	○	△	□	○	△	□	○	△	□
Position Number	1	2	3	4	5	6	7	8	9	10	11	12

a. The given pattern has a cyclic structure. What are the next two shapes in the pattern?

b. What do and should K and first-grade students learn from activities that involve repeating patterns?

c. If you extend the pattern, what shape will be in the 15th position? 18th position? 21st position? 30th position? How is this problem related to the concept of division in third grade, and how does that concept help you determine the shape in any position without having to perform extensive counting?

d. If you extend the pattern, what shape will be in the 16th position? 20th position? 34th position? 127rd position? 2372nd position? How is this problem related to division in fourth grade?

e. Students begin to formally use letter variables in sixth grade. Let the variable n stand for position number. How might a sixth-grade student write a rule that would enable him or her to predict the correct shape in the nth position? Also, establish a rule involving the variable n that describes the general position of the following objects in the string: square, triangle, and circle. How are these tasks related to remainders?

f. Students learn geometric transformations in a plane in eighth grade. Refer to p. 75 of the CCSSM to learn something about them. Find an alternative way of describing repeating patterns in terms of transformations.
g. Describe everyday instances of repeating patterns that are appropriate at each grade level from kindergarten to fifth grade.

2.7 REASONING AND PROOF IN ELEMENTARY SCHOOL MATHEMATICS

Knowing how to reason (and prove) mathematically is just as equally important as knowing how to process problems deductively by applying the appropriate rules. Work through the following activity below with a partner.

2.7.1 Content Activity 7: Division Problems in Third Grade

Think about how you might obtain the quotient of each third-grade division problem below? Share your work with a partner and carefully pay attention to each other's explanations.

$$3\overline{)36}, \ 3\overline{)27}, \text{ and } 3\overline{)96}.$$

Refer to standards **3.OA.3**, **3.OA.6**, and **3.OA.7**. How are third grade students expected to reason about dividing whole numbers within 100? Do you see similarities between everyday reasoning about division problems and the mathematical explanation? When third-grade students explain how they obtain such quotients, what does "explain" mean in their context?

Reasoning and proof are fundamentally, tied to beliefs. When students reason, they convey beliefs that are usually based on inferential norms that are appropriate at their level of experience. Certainly, those beliefs will evolve over time depending on how well they are able to coordinate factors relevant to perceptual and conceptual competence and representational ability.

– *Perceptual competence* involves making inferences on the basis of what one sees at the moment.
– *Conceptual competence* involves making analytical inferences on the basis of one's ability to interpret valid mathematical relationships, properties, features, or attributes of objects beyond the limits of perceptual competence.
– *Representational ability* involves employing gestures, drawing pictures and diagrams, and using abstract entities (numeric forms, variables, and combinations) that enable one to externalize concepts and percepts.

Reasoning and proof activities help deepen elementary students' developing mathematical understanding. Activities that encourage them to generate propositions or conjectures and claims or provide explanations that justify their truth values (e.g.: why they are either true or false; how they are true or false; under what conditions they are either true or false) help them establish certainty and necessity in their developing mathematical knowledge. Many of them, of course, tend to reason through examples that are intended to empirically demonstrate certainty at their level of experience. Further, the examples they use and the repeated stable actions that come with them convey how they sense and capture the necessity of an interpreted structure. Consider the following second-grade activity that involves the parity concept (i.e., evenness or oddness) of whole numbers (**2.OA.3**).

2.7.2 Activity 8: Even and Odd Numbers in Second Grade

a. How might you introduce the concept of even and odd (whole) numbers to second-grade students?
b. If you are unable to provide an answer to (a), think of an even number in terms of a pair of circles or sticks. Think of an odd number as a pair of circles or sticks with a leftover circle or stick. Demonstrate these representations several times with larger numbers.
c. Try to think at the level of a second-grade student who is learning the concept of parity for the first time. Obtain a mathematical conjecture for each problem situation below and find a way to prove your conjecture (i.e., it is always true).

   – Add two even whole numbers. What is the parity of the sum? How do you know for sure?
   – Add two odd whole numbers. What is the parity of the sum? How do you know for sure?
   – Add an even number and an odd number. What is the parity of the sum? How do you know for sure?

d. How might a second-grade student accomplish the following task: *A friend of yours claims that the sum of an even number and an odd number is even. What do you tell your friend about her claim?*

In task (d), providing several examples may be used as a reasoning strategy. However, students need to know that they only need one example in order to show that the claim is false (i.e., a *counterexample*).

Consider the following task below. How might second-grade students use examples of whole numbers to establish and justify the parity of the whole number zero?

e. Is 0 (zero) even or odd? How do you know for sure?

When you teach elementary school students to reason mathematically, you should help them develop competence in three different kinds of explanations, as follows:

– *Abductive reasoning*, which involves forming conjectures or claims;

23

– *Inductive reasoning*, which involves performing repeated actions as a way of demonstrating the empirical validity of conjectures or claims;
– *Reasoning that emerges from a deductive argument*, which involves using abductive and inductive claims together as hypotheses in order to implement a valid mathematical action (e.g., a rule).

For example, consider the following steps that demonstrate the parity of the sum of any pair of even whole numbers.

   I. $2 + 2 = 4$. The sum is even.
  II. $4 + 6 = 10$. The sum is even.
 III. $2 + 8 = 10$. The sum is even.
 IV. $6 + 6 = 12$. The sum is even.
  V. Two even addends yield a sum that is even.
 VI. So $26 + 12$, which equals 38, should be even.

Each claim under steps I, II, III, and IV closes with an abduction, that is, a guess or conjecture. Steps I through IV support step V, which illustrates an instance of inductive reasoning. Step VI involves reasoning that emerges from the preceding five steps; it exemplifies what is called a *deductively-closed argument* that is empirically supported by both abduction and induction. When you ask elementary students to reason about mathematical objects and relationships, you should aim to have them establish deductive closure at all times, which is a fundamental characteristic of the analytical condition of mathematical representations. Work with a pair and deal with the following two questions below.

f. What happens when elementary school students are not provided with sufficient opportunities to engage in abductive and inductive reasoning?
g. What happens when elementary school students are able to exhibit abductive and inductive reasoning but unable to achieve deductive closure?

2.8 COMMUNICATION IN ELEMENTARY SCHOOL MATHEMATICS

When you ask elementary students to communicate in the mathematics classroom, it means that you want them to pay serious attention to forming, using, reasoning with, and connecting various forms of representations. Communication enables them to externalize an idea in some recognizable form for personal and public access. Personal access is a form of intra-communication that helps them monitor what and how they are thinking when they are in the process of conceptualizing or problem solving. However, meaningful communication takes place in a public domain, where individuals have access to each other's representations. Hence, public access is a form of inter-communication that helps them monitor and learn from each other with the goal of developing shared intent, knowledge, and practices over time. Meaningful communication in public also targets the development of more refined and sophisticated forms of representation and reasoning, including the relevant connections that make them interesting. Further, because personal communication of mathematical representations among young children is often course and situated, their experiences in public communication provide them with structured opportunities that enable them to negotiate and bridge conceptual and representational gaps between personal and formal or institutional versions. This purposeful public communication in mathematical activity fosters the emergence of exact and valid forms of representations.

The initial forms of public communication among young children tend to be verbal, gestural, pictorial, or reflect combinations of at least two forms. They also rely on manipulatives and other concrete tools to help them communicate. Consider Content Activity 1, which involves the problem of constructing addition facts to 10 in a kindergarten class. Some students who are proficient in English (or in an official language) are often able to verbalize their responses. In some cases, their verbal responses are accompanied by stories that may or may not be relevant to the intended solutions. Among English learners, including children who are not ready to talk in public, they are likely to employ gestures or draw pictures. For example, some first-grade students might perform addition and subtraction to 10 by using their fingers, counting with unit cubes, or drawing detailed pictures of objects that convey various processes of counting all, counting on, and counting backward.

Verbal, gestural, and pictorial means of public communication should be supported, of course. However, they are good tools to think with but only when children are able to extract the analytical conditions of representations. Think about the following task below and discuss your responses with a pair.

2.8.1 Content Activity 9: Addition and Subtraction Strategies from First to Second Grade

a. Focus on Content Activity 1 once again. What meaningful gestural actions will support growth in K students' developing understanding of addition facts? Which ones will they be able to use when they deal with larger numbers in first grade ?
b. Think about how first-grade students might add the following numbers in the absence of any formal intervention: $5 + 3$, $3 + 5$, $8 + 6$, $6 + 8$, $12 + 2$, $2 + 12$, $3 + 17$, $11 + 5$. What meaningful verbal and/or gestural representations will help them deal with all addition problems to 20 in a structural manner (**1.OA.6**)?
c. Think about how first-grade students might perform subtraction on each of the following sets of problems in the absence of any formal intervention:

    Set I: $5 - 3$, $8 - 4$, $9 - 6$, $10 - 5$, $7 - 4$
    Set II: $12 - 2$, $18 - 10$, $20 - 15$, $11 - 9$, $20 - 12$

What meaningful verbal, gestural, and pictorial representations will help them deal with each type of subtraction problems to 20 (**1.OA.6**)? What is the purpose of categorizing subtraction problems to 20 into two sets?

Writing solutions is the most significant form of public communication in mathematics. Among elementary students, it involves drawing pictures and diagrams, setting up number expressions and number sentences (i.e., equations and inequalities), graphing mathematical relationships, constructing tables of values, etc. Unlike verbal and gesture-driven solutions as forms of communication, however, having them write their solutions involves asking them to externalize in paper their understanding "all aspects relevant to language use, from vocabulary and syntax to the development and organization of ideas" (NGSS/CCSS, 2011, p. 19). Further, "a key purpose of writing is to communicate clearly to an external, sometimes unfamiliar audience" and "begin to adapt the form and content of their writing to accomplish a particular task and purpose" (ibid, p. 18). While these perspectives on writing have been taken from the appropriate sections in the *Common Core State Standards for English Language Arts and Literacy in History/Social Studies, Science, and Technical Subjects*, they also apply to writing solutions in school mathematics.

When you ask elementary students to write solutions to mathematical problems, your most significant task involves helping them coordinate the following actions below, which they need to clearly manifest in order to develop a good writing structure.

– *Processing action*, which involves drawing pictures and diagrams that show how they perceive relationships in a problem.
– *Translating action*, which involves converting the processing action in correct mathematical form.

Certainly, some, if not most, students will talk and employ gestures when they either draw pictures or use their fingers to count. But having them draw pictures help them make the transition to the formal phase of writing. Pictures evolve much later into diagrams with increased conceptual competence. Pictures are iconic forms of representation, meaning they remain faithful to the depicted objects. For example, a word problem that involves apples might yield a written solution with drawn apples. Diagrams are either indexical or symbolic forms of representation. Indexical forms are figures that emerge out of association, while symbolic forms are figures that emerge from shared rules of discourse. For example, the long division form shown in section 2.7.1, which involves a right parenthesis (or in many textbooks a straight vertical segment) with an attached vinculum that extends to the right, is not symbolic but indexical since the form reminds children to perform division. Variables such as X, Y, and Z are symbols that the mathematics community employ to fulfill certain purposes.

Kindergarten through second grade students like to draw iconic pictures that contain features that are irrelevant to a problem, so they will need time to process the problem. However, with appropriate scaffolding, they can be taught to transform those pictures into diagrams. Indexical and symbolic diagrams can be mere skeletal shapes of figures or placeholder figures and do not need to resemble the original source.

A good example of a transition from pictures to diagrams involves the place value structure of whole numbers (**K.NBT.1**, **1.NBT.2**, **2.NBT.1**, and **3.NBT.1**). Elementary students from kindergarten to third grade are usually taught to represent whole numbers with the Dienes blocks, shown in Figure 2.4, where a unit cube stands for 1, a long stands for a bundle of ten 10 unit cubes, a flat stands for a bundle of 10 longs, and a cube stands for a bundle of 10 flats. When they start to draw longs and flats, in particular, they usually take their time to draw stacks of squares. Doing that helps them remember the values associated with each term and the corresponding values. Over time, however, they can be taught to simplify those pictures by drawing sticks and squares to represent longs and flats, respectively, and with circles corresponding to unit cubes for ones as shown in Figure 2.4. The California-adopted Singapore elementary textbooks consistently use labeled circle representations that show powers of ten ($1 = 10^0$, $10 = 10^1$, $100 = 10^2$, $1000 = 10^3$, etc.) as shown in Figure 2.4.

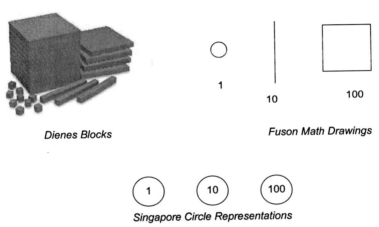

Dienes Blocks   Fuson Math Drawings

Singapore Circle Representations

Figure 2.4. Visual-based place value representations of whole numbers

Elementary students are naturally drawn to process mathematical problems due to the interesting contexts in which they arise or are framed. However, many of them often find it difficult to convert their processing actions in correct and acceptable mathematical form. Explore the following activity below. Pay attention to potential issues in processing and converting representations in first grade.

2.8.2 Content Activity 10: Generating Addition and Subtraction Facts in First Grade

Work with a pair to accomplish the following mathematical activity below that involves asking first-grade students to establish a relationship between addition and subtraction (e.g., $6 + 4 = 10$, $10 - 4 = 6$, and $10 - 6 = 4$ are all equivalent number facts; **1.OA.6**). Answer the questions that follow.

d. For each set of numbers, generate an addition fact and the corresponding subtraction facts.

Set I: 3, 6, 9
Set II: 12, 7, 19
Set III: 19, 1, 20

27

e. How did you process the task? Did your processing help you convert or translate your solutions in mathematical form?

f. How might first-grade students be taught to coordinate their processing and translating actions so that they understand the conceptual relationship between addition and subtraction? What meaningful representations are appropriate at their grade level? Proceed to (g) if you need more assistance.

g. Figure 2.5 shows a diagram that can help first-grade students process and convert the given task in mathematical form. The diagram is often referred to as a *math triangle*. The example illustrates an addition-subtraction math triangle for the triad of 2, 3, and 5.

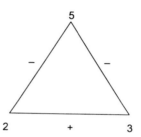

Figure 2.5. Addition/Subtraction math triangle

Name an addition fact and the two corresponding subtraction facts.

What makes the diagram in Figure 2.5 a helpful tool in children's processing and translating actions relevant to the **1.OA.6** standard?

How can you use math triangle diagrams to help third-grade students understand the conceptual relationship between multiplication and division?

2.9 DOING MATHEMATICS WITH AN EYE ON THE CONTENT-PRACTICE STANDARDS OF THE CCSSM

Hopefully the preceding sections have given you sufficient and meaningful insights and experiences that encouraged you to reflect on how you might begin to structure content teaching and learning with the practice standards in mind. You will learn more about the relationship between content and practice standards in the next seven chapters that focus on the core domains in the CCSSM elementary school mathematics curriculum. *Domains* consist of *clusters* – organized groups – of related standards, where each *standard* defines in explicit terms what elementary students need to understand and be able to do. The six elementary domains in the CCSSM are as follows:

– Counting and cardinality in kindergarten;
– Operations and algebraic thinking from kindergarten to Grade 5;

- Whole numbers and operations in base 10 from kindergarten to Grade 5;
- Fractions and operations from Grade 1 to Grade 5;
- Measurement and data from kindergarten to Grade 5; and
- Geometry from kindergarten to Grade 5;

An example of a cluster of three standards under the *CCSSM Counting and Cardinality* domain is shown in Figure 2.6.

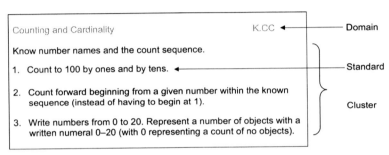

Figure 2.6. CCSSM format

Figure 2.2 is an interpretive visual model of the eight practice standards. While the CCSSM considers all practices as essential, the perspective that is assumed in this book embraces a stronger position. The solid triangle in Figure 2.2 conveys three essential mathematical practices that all students need to seriously consider each time they learn mathematical content. Having a positive disposition towards mathematical problems and problem solving is central. Knowing which tools to use, formal or informal, and when to use them further support and strengthen that disposition. Also, given the symbolic nature of school mathematical content, which is both formal and exact, attending to precision at all times introduces an algebraic disposition towards tool use in which case emerging and meaningful symbols convey expressions that are certain and necessary in the long term. Any of the remaining practice standards can then be coupled with the solid triangle depending on the goals of mathematical activity.

Work with a pair and accomplish the following two activities below.

First, access the following link, which describes in detail the eight practice standards in the CCSSM: http://www.corestandards.org/Math/Practice. For each practice standard, develop a checklist of specific actions that is appropriate for elementary students. Some statements under each practice standard may not be appropriate for kindergarten to Grade 5 students, so consult with each other and decide which ones matter. You may refer to Table 2.3 for a sample of a beginning checklist structure for Practice Standard 1.

Second, in this chapter you explored ten content activities. Use the checklist in Table 2.4 to determine which practice standards apply under each content activity.

When you teach with a content-practice perspective, remember that you (and your colleagues) decide which practice standards to emphasize over others, which you should then carefully align with your teaching, learning, and assessment plans.

Table 2.3. Sample of a Beginning Checklist of Actions for Practice Standard 1

	Practice Standard 1: *Make sense of problems and persevere in solving them.* Provide elementary students with every opportunity to –
1.1	start by explaining to themselves the meaning of a problem and looking for entry points to its solution.
1.2	analyze givens, constraints, relationships, and goals.
1.3	
1. 4	
1.5	
etc.	

Table 2.4. Practice Standards Checklist for the 10 Content Activities in this chapter ("PS" means "Practice Standard")

Content Activity	PS 1	PS 2	PS 3	PS 4	PS 5	PS 6	PS 7	PS 8
Generating Addition Facts								
Building a Hexagon Flower Garden Design								
Different Types of Problems in Elementary School Mathematics								
Kindergarten Subtraction Task								
Representing Whole Numbers in Second Grade								
Repeating Patterns								
Division Problems in Third Grade								
Even and Odd Numbers in Second Grade								
Addition and Subtraction Strategies from First to Second Grade								
Generating Addition and Subtraction Facts in First Grade								

COUNTING AND CARDINALITY IN KINDERGARTEN

In this chapter, you will explore content-practice, teaching, and learning issues relevant to the *Counting and Cardinality* domain in the kindergarten (K) CCSSM. Table 3.1 shows the three clusters that comprise this domain, representing the seven individual content standards that every K student needs to learn by the end of the school year. At the very least, the content standards provide all K students with a strong foundation for developing early structure sense. In the context of counting activity, they begin to establish regularities in the way whole numbers up to 100 are represented, that is, named, said, and written down in paper. Remember that content standards are meant to be taught throughout the entire school year, meaning to say that each standard or a set of standards drawn from either a cluster or across the three clusters is expected to spiral over instructional time.

3.1 SUBITIZING: LAYING THE FOUNDATION FOR EARLY MULTIPLICATIVE THINKING

All K students need to become proficient subitizers in order to experience success in counting small and large whole numbers. Whole numbers consist of 0 and the natural numbers 1, 2, 3, 4, 5, …. *Subitizing* is an ability to engage in a quick, confident, and correct judgment of cardinality relative to a set of objects. *Cardinality* refers to the number of objects in the set regardless of the order in which they appear (**K.CC.4b**).

There are two levels of subitizing that all K children should be able to exhibit in order to do well in first grade and beyond, as follows:

– *Perceptual subitizing*, which involves quickly establishing the cardinality of very small sets of objects, say, 1 to 4, without resorting to a counting-all strategy;
– *Analytical subitizing*, which involves quickly counting in terms of familiar groups (or units) without resorting to a counting-all strategy.

Notice that if you raise two of your fingers or see a picture with two dots in whatever arrangement you see them, you do not count all from 1. Instead, you have a perception of seeing them together, enabling you to instantly claim the cardinality of 2. Such competence in subitizing marks the beginning stage of multiplicative thinking because you see objects together as one unit. K students who employ a counting all action exhibit *additive thinking* in which case they see objects in a set as separate and unrelated from each other. So, in the case of the two raised fingers or the picture with two dots, they will say, "1, 2." Try to interview a K student. Show a picture with 4 dots and assess whether the student exhibits perceptual subitizing.

Table 3.1. Counting and Cardinality Standards for Kindergarten Mathematics

Counting and Cardinality	K.CC

Know number names and the count sequence.

1.   Count to 100 by ones and by tens.
2.   Count forward beginning from a given number within the known sequence (instead of having to begin at 1).
3.   Write numbers from 0 to 20. Represent a number of objects with a written numeral 0-20 (with 0 representing a count of no objects).

Count to tell the number of objects.

4.   Understand the relationship between numbers and quantities; connect counting to cardinality.
   a.   When counting objects, say the number names in the standard order, pairing each object with one and only one number name and each number name with one and only one object.
   b.   Understand that the last number name said tells the number of objects counted. The number of objects is the same regardless of their arrangement or the order in which they were counted.
   c.   Understand that each successive number name refers to a quantity that is one larger.
5.   Count to answer "how many?" questions about as many as 20 things arranged in a line, a rectangular array, or a circle, or as many as 10 things in a scattered configuration; given a number from 1–20, count out that many objects.

Compare numbers.

6.   Identify whether the number of objects in one group is greater than, less than, or equal to the number of objects in another group, e.g., by using matching and counting strategies.1
7.   Compare two numbers between 1 and 10 presented as written numerals.

All K students will also need to learn to coordinate both physical and linguistic representations of counting number. The initial disposition towards counting all, in fact, provides them with an opportunity to rehearse the number names in sequence. Over time, however, the physical and linguistic pairing should become automatic. This is a nonnegotiable condition for counting at the K level.

Numbers are ideas, while numerals are cultural and shared representations of numbers. In actual practice, the two terms are used interchangeably. One well-known and widely accepted number system consists of *decimal (Indo-Arabic) numerals*, and it uses the famous ten single digits from 0, 1, 2, 3, ..., to 9. Central to the concept of whole numbers that all K students need to acquire is a *splitting structure* called *place value*, which requires multiplicative thinking. Teaching and learning issues relevant to place value structures are discussed in Chapter 4. For now, look at Figure 3.1. What whole number does it represent?

Figure 3.1. A visual depiction of a whole number

If your quick response was 14, you just exhibited analytical subitizing. You might have seen two sets, a group of 10 and a group of 4, in which case your multiplicative thinking ability facilitated the subitizing process. Try the activity with a K student and determine whether the student exhibits additive or multiplicative thinking.

K students need to learn to analytically subitize because it will support them once they begin to explore mathematics in terms of *structures*. If you show them your left hand (or a five-frame) and, much later, both hands (or a ten-frame), having analytical subitizing proficiency should help them quickly say "five" and "ten," respectively, without having to spend a considerable amount of time engaging in counting all action. Analytical subitizing is also a nonnegotiable condition for counting at the K level that supports efficient counting to 100 by ones and by tens (**K.CC.1**).

The following link below will prepare you to teach perceptual subitizing to K students. Work with a pair and do the activities. Then answer the questions that follow.

http://www.edplus.canterbury.ac.nz/literacy_numeracy/maths/numdocuments/
dot_card_and_ten_frame_package2005.pdf

a. Share with your pair activities that you like the most and the least, and why.
b. Generate other physical tools that you can use to help K students develop proficiency in subitizing.
c. Search the internet for free online apps and games relevant to perceptual and analytical subitizing and assess potential benefits and possible concerns.

3.2 COUNTING AND WRITING NUMBERS AND NUMBER WORDS: BUILDING ON
RHYTHMIC STRUCTURES

Daily and repetitive activities in counting numbers to 100 by ones and by tens can facilitate the mutual coordination of, and correspondences between, the physical and linguistic representations of number among K students (**K.CC.4a**). The coordinated representation is an individual developmental phenomenon, which explains why you need to be ready to differentiate instruction if it becomes necessary. By differentiating instruction, it means designing instruction in such a way that meets the individual needs of students with the explicit goal of helping all of them achieve the same goal. K students progress individually depending on cognitive, social, and cultural factors that influence their choices, actions, and decisions. Hence, when they engage in counting activity at least in the beginning phase of learning about whole numbers, they will most likely manifest different types and levels of proficiencies and competencies. Below are a few typical classroom tools that you can use to help K children count to 100 by tens and by ones.

- Hundreds chart, http://illuminations.nctm.org/lessons/HundredsChart.pdf
- Number line, http://www.sparklebox.co.uk/maths/counting/number-lines/number-lines.html#.UZTBhHBQ50p
- Counting songs, http://www.goorulearning.org/gooru/index.g#!/resource/counting%201%20to%2010%20song/search (from 1 to 10), http://www.youtube.com/watch?v=Zw6Fps2O7XY (from 1 to 20)

In the case of the hundreds chart and the number line, you may need to make individual copies and tape them onto every child's desk for open access. They are helpful to K students especially when they begin to count forward from a number other than 1 (K.CC.2). In the case of the hundreds chart, you may use (magnetic) unit cubes to fill in each box for each day that they go to school, which you can then use as an occasion to engage in counting all action in the standard order (K.CC.4a and K.CC.1) and pose the "how many" question (K.CC.5).

Helping K students become fully aware of rhythm in their utterances when they count by tens and by ones can also help them later when they begin to conceptualize numbers in terms of structures. Rhythm supports the emergence of structure sense about number names. Take, for instance, counting to 100 by tens. Access the link below. Notice that in the case of the –*ty* numbers, what is said is linked to two written representations. Eventually, any mention of "ty" conjures an image of a number than ends in 0. The "–*ty*" rhythm becomes K students' cue that should then assist them in writing the correct numeral. Having the list on the right of Figure 3.2 in a poster on a classroom wall further reinforces mastery of the decade sequence of numbers.

http://www.goorulearning.org/gooru/index.g#!/r/29071c65-bbcb-4fd6-8adc-c6d2f82bcda3

The same rhythmic approach can be used to help K students remember the –*teen* numbers. Having the list on the left of Figure 3.2 in a poster on a classroom wall them see the connections among the different representations of the –*teen* numbers.

-Teen Numbers			-Ty Numbers			
1 teen	eleven	11	1 ten		ten	10
2 teen	twelve	12	2 ten	2 ty	twenty	20
3 teen	thirteen	13	3 ten	3 ty	thirty	30
4 teen	fourteen	14	4 ten	4 ty	forty	40
5 teen	fifteen	15	5 ten	5 ty	fifty	50
6 teen	sixteen	16	6 ten	6 ty	sixty	60
7 teen	seventeen	17	7 ten	7 ty	seventy	70
8 teen	eighteen	18	8 ten	8 ty	eighty	80
9 teen	nineteen	19	9 ten	9 ty	ninety	90

Figure 3.2. The structures of the –teen and the –ty numbers

Work with a pair and discuss the following questions below.

a. Which –ty and –teen numbers do you anticipate K children will have difficulty remembering, and why? Ask K teachers or seek resources online that will help you deal with such potential difficulties.
b. One potential difficulty that K students might have when they count numbers to 100 invoves making the transition from the –nine to the –ty (e.g.: twenty-nine to thirty, forty-nine to fifty). Find ways that will help you deal with this transition difficulty.
c. K students are expected to write numerals and represent a number of objects with a written numeral within 20. Find resources can you use and/or develop to help them succeed on such tasks.

While the CCSSM recommends having K students write numbers from 0 to 20 (**K.CC.3**), it does not say anything about writing number words, which is another form of written representation. In the event that you have K students who are ready to write number words, one effective support involves providing them with laminated number cards. Figure 3.3 shows a front-and-back sample of a page that has the numerals 1 to 6 appearing on one side and the corresponding number words appearing on the other side of the page. Make number cards from 0 to 20. Assemble the cards and then use a screw lock ring to bind them together.

1	4
2	5
3	6

Four	One
Five	Two
Six	Three

Figure 3.3. Number cards

3.3 COMPARING QUANTITIES

Before K students learn to count in exact terms, they possess an informal sense of the meanings of certain protoquantitative terms such as *more, less, bigger,* and *smaller* that convey global and approximate feature of objects and sets of objects. Your job is to introduce them to the meaning of *quantities* in mathematics. That is, while cardinality refers to counting, which produces a number, *quantity* refers to both cardinality and unit of count (**K.CC.4**). For example, Figure 3.4 shows 3 umbrellas, where the number 3 refers to the cardinality and umbrella is the unit of count.

Why is the mathematical concept of quantity necessary in the K mathematics curriculum? At the very least, K students need to understand that the mathematical process of comparing involves the assumption of having a common unit of

Figure 3.4 A Picture of 3 Umbrellas

Figure 3.5. A picture of umbrellas that convey more umbrellas on the left than on the right

comparison. For example, in Figure 3.5, it is easy to see that there are more objects on the left than on the right because the implied or taken-for-granted context involves a common unit, umbrellas. The process of matching or comparing can then assist them in translating or converting their response in mathematical form, $3 > 2$.

However, they also need to understand that any comparison task involving two or more sets of objects means identifying a unit that is a shared feature of all the the objects in both sets. For example, in Figure 3.6, the translated mathematical statement

$$9 > 4$$

really means

$$9 \text{ objects} > 4 \text{ objects,}$$

where "objects" pertain to a common feature (i.e., unit) of the two sets of things.

Hence, when K student compare sets of objects, they need to acquire the mathematical understanding that the relational terms "greater than," "less than," and "equal to" assume a sound conceptual grasp of quantities and common units in order to make the matching process meaningful and sensible to start with. Standard **K.CC.6** assumes the common unit *object*, which simplifies the process of comparing and matching for K students. The same assumption holds for standard **K.CC.7**, which focuses on comparing two numbers presented as written numerals (e.g.: 7 ? 4; 2 ? 5; 3 ? 3).

It should also be noted that the foregoing conception of quantities supports growth in multiplicative and structural thinking, which are core mathematical abilities that all students must develop proficiently in order to experience long-term success in the subject.

36

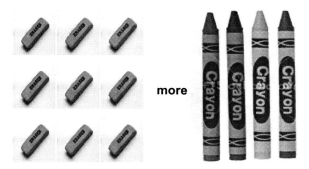

Figure 3.6. A picture of objects that illustrates 9 > 4

3.4 MAPPING THE CONTENT STANDARDS WITH THE PRACTICE STANDARDS

Work with a pair and accomplish the following two tasks below.

a. Use the checklist you developed in Table 2.3 to map each content standard under the *Counting and Cardinality* domain with the appropriate practice standards. Use the structure shown in Table 3.2 to record your responses.
b. Determine which among the five NRC proficiency strands (see Table 2.2) can be used to learn each content standard. Remember that the strands, like the CCSSM practice standards, should not be interpreted as single stand-alone proficiencies. Since they target different dimensions of mathematical learning, using several strands in mathematical activity will help strengthen students' mathematical proficiency.

3.5 DEVELOPING A CONTENT STANDARD PROGRESSION TABLE FOR THE COUNTING AND CARDINALITY DOMAIN

Work on your own to develop a reasonable content standard progression table for this particular domain (i.e., a domain table) over a course of nine months. A *content standard progression* is a gradual development of a content standard from the relatively simple case(s) to the target case(s) over time. For example, the second row in Table 3.3 shows a content progression for the standard "Count to 100 by ones and by tens (K.CC.1)" that all students learn over 9 months. For the first four months, K students will learn to count up to 30 by tens and by ones. The range increases each month until the target grade-level cardinality is achieved. A domain table should show the different content standard progressions and their interrelationships over time. You may use the table shown in Table 3.3 for a beginning structure. Remember that progressions and domain tables are negotiated in actual practice (i.e., either at the school or district level). This activity should prepare you for instructional planning, which you will pursue in detail in Chapter 12.

Table 3.2. Mapping Counting and Cardinality Domain to the Practice Standards and Proficiency Strands

CCSSM Content Standards	CCSSM Practice Standards								NRC Mathematical Proficiency Strands				
	Make sense of problems and persevere in solving them	Reason abstractly and quantitatively	Construct viable arguments and critique the reasoning of others	Model with mathematics	Use appropriate tools strategically	Attend to precision	Look for and make use of structure	Look for and express regularity in repeated reasoning	Conceptual understanding	Procedural fluency	Strategic competence	Adaptive reasoning	Productive disposition
K.CC.1													
K.CC.2													
K.CC.3													
K.CC.4													
K.CC.5													
K.CC.6													
K.CC.7													

Table 3.3. A Content Standard Progression Table for the Counting and Cardinality Domain

CCSM Content Standards	September	October	November	December	January	February	March	April	May	June
K.CC.1	Count to 10.	Count to 20 by tens and by ones.	Count to 20 by tens and by ones.	Count to 30 by tens and by ones.	Count to 40 by tens and by ones.	Count to 50 by tens and by ones.	Count to 60 by tens and by ones.	Count to 80 by tens and by ones.	Count to 100 by tens and by ones.	Review
K.CC.2										
K.CC.3										
...										
K.CC.7										

39

NUMBERS AND OPERATIONS (PART I)

In this chapter, you will deal with content-practice, teaching, and learning issues relevant to the place value structure of whole numbers and decimal numbers up to the thousandths place in the *Number and Operations in Base Ten (NBT)* domain from kindergarten (K) through Grade 5 of the CCSSM. Table 4.1 lists the appropriate pages for your convenience. In Chapter 6, you will deal with whole numbers and decimal numbers again but in the context of the four fundamental operations. Remember that the *Counting and Cardinality* domain in Chapter 3 is strongly connected to the NBT domain in this chapter, meaning to say that K through Grade 5 students need to have proficiency in both domains in order to have a solid understanding of whole numbers and decimal numbers, their properties, and the four arithmetical operations.

Table 4.1. CCSSM Pages for the NBT Domain

Grade Level Domain	Standards	Page Numbers in the CCSSM
K.NBT	1	12
1.NBT	1 to 6	15-16
2.NBT	1 to 4	19
3.NBT	1 to 3	24
4.NBT	1 to 6	29-30
5.NBT	1 to 7	35

Take a moment to learn a few things about what the *NBT* standards say about whole numbers and decimal numbers by grade level. Make a wordle by listing down NBT-related terms and other words that you find pertinent and important for K through 5 students to know. Access the link http://www.wordle.net/ to create a wordle. In the box where it tells you to "paste in a bunch of text," repetitions of the same word are allowed and should, thus, be recorded as many times as they appear in the domain. For example, the word "number" is a frequent term, so record the word each time you see it mentioned. When you are done constructing your own *NBT* wordle, share it with others. Which terms appear to be more prominent than others?

4.1 PLACE VALUE IN BASE TEN: THE BASIC MATHEMATICAL STRUCTURE OF WHOLE NUMBERS AND DECIMAL NUMBERS IN THE CCSSM

By the end fifth grade, all elementary students should know that the mathematical structure of whole numbers and decimal numbers involves place value in base 10. That is, the explicit rule or procedure for organizing and counting objects in a set involves forming groups of 1, 10, 100, 1000, and so on. For example, a set of 15 objects is (mentally) seen in terms of 1 group of ten objects and 5 remaining objects, while 15 groups of 10 objects (i.e., a set of 150 objects) are further interpreted in terms of 1 group of 100 objects and 5 groups of 10 objects. Consequently, the place value structure of any whole number in base 10 assigns a value to every digit in the number, which is determined by its position within the whole number. For example, the number 123 has a ones place, a tens place, and a hundreds place from right to left. The digit 1 has a value of 1 hundred, 2 has a value of 2 tens, and 3 has a value of 3 ones. All students need to learn and get used to the term *digit* in a number. The term comes from the Latin word *digitus,* meaning "finger."

There are two basic issues that you need to explicitly address when your students are beginning to learn how to write and say numbers in base 10, as follows:

1. Some students may confuse place value with value (e.g., the value of 1 in 123 is 1).
2. Some students may experience dfficulty saying and writing numbers in the following two cases below.
   a. The –ty and the –teen numbers (e.g., thirty and thirteen)
   b. The missing digit (e.g., one hundred and two appears as 12 in written form)

The term *decimal* should be introduced early. Both the term and the underlying structure are necessary and prominent in fifth grade when students learn the base-10 place value structure formally in terms of powers of 10 (**5.NBT**). In fifth grade, they are also introduced to the term *decimal system*, which conveys a very convenient and well-defined mathematical structure that employs multiplicative thinking since the systematic recording of the cardinalities of groups of objects are accomplished in bundles of 10. Work with a pair to do the following tasks below.

a. Investigate the NBT domain in relation to the decimal numeral system. How is it expected to evolve from kindergarten to fifth grade?
b. Engage in a historical analysis of the term *decimal*. Name everyday and other mathematical situations that use the term *deci*. Discuss advantages and disadvantages of the decimal numeral system.
c. Focus on cluster **5.NBT**. Fifth-grade students learn the term *powers of 10* in relation to the expanded form of whole numbers and decimal numbers. How do numbers appear in base 2? in base 5? in base 7? What are the acceptable digits in base 10, and and how come? Name the acceptable digits in base 2, base 5, and base 7, and how many in each case. Establish a generalization that applies to any base.

4.2 REPRESENTING WHOLE NUMBERS IN BASE TEN FROM K TO GRADE 4

Work with a pair and explore the following questions below.

a. Focus on **K.NBT.1**. How does the process of grouping of objects from 11 to 19 (or, better yet, 10 to 20) facilitate K students' early understanding of place value? What can they learn from composing and decomposing numbers up to 19?

b. Focus on **1.NBT.1**. Design counting sequence problems that will help first-grade students learn to count, read, and write numbers in both numerical and word forms.

c. Focus on **1.NBT.2** and **2.NBT.1**. Also, refer to Figure 2.4. Discuss advantages and disadvantages of each visual system of place value representations for whole numbers.

d. Students continue to learn place value representations in third grade using various representations such as those shown in Figure 2.4. Moving on to fourth grade, consider **4.NBT.1**. What mathematical concepts are necessary to help students see sensible relationships between two or more power-of-10 values?

e. Focus on **2.NBT.3**, **4.NBT.3**, and **5.NBT.3a**. Develop a graphic organizer that will help students to see equivalent representations of whole numbers (number in base-10 numeral form, diagram form, number word/name, expanded form, and place-value chart).

f. Express 1 trillion as a power of 10 (i.e., of the form 10^n, where n is a whole number). Access the following site to help you gain visual access to one trillion dollars beginning with a \$100 bill: http://www.pagetutor.com/trillion/index.html. How can this activity help fifth grade students learn important relationships regarding powers of 10 and, more generally, powers of any whole number?

g. Search the internet for free online apps and games that deal with whole numbers and place value. Assess potential benefits and possible concerns.

4.3 REPRESENTING DECIMAL NUMBERS IN GRADE 5

Continue working with a pair and explore the following questions below.

a. Focus on **5.NBT.1** and **5.NBT.3a**. How does knowing **4.NBT.1** help students construct the place value structure of decimal numbers? What additional mathematical concepts are necessary in describing this structure?

Students first learn about decimals in second grade when they solve word problems involving dollar bills, quarters, dimes, nickels, and pennies with the appropriate symbols (**2.MD.8**). Compare that context with the one that is suggested for fifth grade students.

2. Using an empty hundreds chart and a colored pencil can help students visualize whole numbers to 100. Access the following link to download an empty hundreds

chart: http://www.eduplace.com/state/pdf/hmm/trb/2/2_11.pdf. Use the chart and a colored pencil to illustrate the number 65 on the chart.

This time assume that each box in a whole empty hundreds chart consists of hundredths instead of ones. How can you use the hundredths chart to help fifth grade students visually understand the meanings of tenths and hundredths? Illustrate 0.10 and 0.01 on the same hundredths chart. Do the same for the numbers 0.5 and 0.05.

c. Some teachers strongly recommend students read decimal numbers as decimal fractions. Below are a few examples.

0.5	"five tenths" and not "zero point five"
3.4	"three and 4 tenths" and not "3.4"
0.25	"twenty-five hundredths" or "two tenths and 5 hundredths" and not "zero point 25"

What do students learn from this particular approach to reading decimal numbers?

d. How can you use an empty hundredths chart to help fifth grade students construct the number 0.005? Visually describe the decimal number 0.235 on the same hundredths chart. Visually describe the difference between 0.1, 0.01, and 0.001 on the same hundredths chart.

What benefits do fifth-grade students obtain from knowing how to visualize decimal numbers?

e. Focus on **5.NBT.3a**. Develop a graphic organizer that will help students to see equivalent representations of decimal numbers (i.e.: number in base-10 numeral form, number name/word, diagram form, expanded form, and place-value chart).

4.4 COMPARING AND ORDERING WHOLE NUMBERS AND DECIMAL NUMBERS FROM GRADES 1 TO 5

Comparing numbers continues to be a core activity in the NBT domain that focuses on whole numbers and decimal numbers. Read content standards **1.NBT.3** and **2.NBT.4** first. Figure 4.1 shows the numbers 35 and 38 in diagrammatic form. How might first-grade students use the stipulated visual representations to help them establish a rule for comparing two or more 2-digit whole numbers? Draw diagrams for the following pairs of whole numbers: 24 and 42; 123 and 128; 204 and 214; 458 and 678. Work with a pair and discuss the following three questions below.

Figure 4.1. Visual representations of 35 and 38

a. What rules emerge from the visual activity of comparing whole numbers? Can students apply the same rules in fifth grade when they deal with decimal numbers (**5.NBT.3b**)?
b. Some students tend to rely heavily on drawing diagrams when they compare two or more whole numbers. Such diagrams help them in their processing, which should not be discouraged. How might you assist them make the transition to rules in the form of algorithms (i.e., stable step-by-step procedures) by drawing on their visual experiences with the diagrams?
c. Focus on **1.NBT.3**. Many students find the inequality symbols > (greater than) and < (less than) confusing and/or difficult to remember. Search online resources that will help them deal with this issue.

4.5 ROUNDING WHOLE NUMBERS FROM GRADES 3 TO 5

Students begin to round whole numbers in third grade (**3.NBT.1**). In fifth grade, they extend rounding activity to include decimal numbers (**5.NBT.4**). Access the following web resources below to learn different rounding approaches. Work with a pair to accomplish the tasks that follow.

– Number line approach, http://www.youtube.com/watch?v=UP7YmXJc7Ik
– Numerical approaches, http://www.mathsisfun.com/rounding-numbers.html
– Practical approaches, http://www.mathcats.com/grownupcats/ideabankrounding. html

a. Develop a poster for rounding whole numbers in third grade.
b. Identify situations in everyday life that support rounding up and rounding down. Why should elementary students need to learn rounding in the first place?
c. When the number to be rounded is exactly a 5, 50, 500, 5000, 50000, and so on, "the" rule is to round up. Explore how this rule is justified and what it means in terms of the types of justification and reasoning that are accepted in mathematics.

4.6 MAPPING THE CONTENT STANDARDS WITH THE PRACTICE STANDARDS

Consistency in task structure will help you develop a solid understanding of the CCSSM framework. The requirements in this section are similar to those listed under section 3.4. Work with a pair and accomplish the following two tasks below.

a. Use the checklist you developed in Table 2.3 to map each content standard under the *NBT Part I* domain with the appropriate practice standards. Make a structure similar to the one shown in Table 3.2 to organize and record your responses.
b. Determine which among the five NRC proficiency strands (see Table 2.2) can be used to help students learn each content standard.

4.7 DEVELOPING A CONTENT STANDARD PROGRESSION TABLE FOR PART I OF THE NUMBERS AND OPERATIONS IN BASE TEN DOMAIN

Choose a grade level between K and Grade 5 that you are interested in exploring in some detail. Develop a nine-month content standard progression table that involves the NBT Part I standards in this chapter. Make sure that your plan is appropriate, reasonable, and logical. Remember that a content standard progression is a gradual development of a content standard over time. Use the structure shown in Table 3.3 to help you organize the different content standard progressions and their possible interrelationships within a timeframe of nine months. If K is your choice of grade level, continue to use Table 3.3 by adding rows corresponding to the NBT Part 1 content standards.

OPERATIONS AND ALGEBRAIC THINKING

In this chapter, you will deal with content-practice, teaching, and learning issues relevant to the *Operations and Algebraic Thinking (OA)* domain from kindergarten (K) through Grade 5 of the CCSSM. Table 5.1 lists the appropriate pages for your convenience. To better appreciate the clusters of content standards that comprise this domain, it is helpful to begin with a clear description of algebra, at least one that is compatible with the CCSSM at the elementary level. This matter is pursued in section 5.1 through Albrecht Heeffer's two views of algebra, one nonsymbolic and the other symbolic. The ideas that are pursued in this section lay the foundation for the remaining sections in this chapter and should help clarify the role of algebra in the other domains of the CCSSM.

At the outset, teaching and learning elementary school mathematics will remain arithmetical, geometrical, and data-analytical in contexts. However, the basic approach that will be used to help students achieve mathematical understanding and proficiency with the relevant rules, processes, and concepts is grounded in a type of algebraic thinking that generates and reasons with deductively-drawn generalizations and structures.

Table 5.1. Page Reference for the OA Domain in the CCSSM

Grade Level Domain	Standards	Page Numbers in the CCSSM
K.OA	1 to 5	11
1.OA	1 to 8	15
2.OA	1 to 4	19
3.OA	1 to 9	23
4.OA	1 to 5	29
5.OA	1 to 3	35

5.1 ALGEBRAIC THINKING FROM KINDERGARTEN TO GRADE 5

Take some time to reflect on your early experiences in mathematics from elementary to high school. As you engage in reflective thinking, access the first three sites below, which capture attitudes that people have in relation to the subject of algebra. Gather at least ten to fifteen more examples online and categorize them in a way that makes sense to you. Assemble them in a mini-poster. When you are done, access the fourth link below, which should take you to Andrew Hacker's controversial July 2012 opinion essay regarding the problematic status of algebra in American education.

- http://luannesmath.files.wordpress.com/2012/07/equation-cartoon.jpg
- http://marklolson.files.wordpress.com/2009/03/sidney-harris-cartoon-a-miracle-occurs-here.gif?w=300&h=364
- http://picrust.files.wordpress.com/2011/08/algebra-cartoon1.jpg
- http://www.nytimes.com/2012/07/29/opinion/sunday/is-algebra-necessary.html?pagewanted=all

Share your poster with a pair and discuss categories and responses that are similar and different. Why does algebra over other mathematics subjects receive so much critical reception from the public that appears to be more negative than positive? What can you do to help change the negative reception towards the subject?

Logician and philosopher of science Albrecht Heeffer's reflections in relation to a recent reinterpretion of early Babylonian problem texts have led him to to suggest two views of algebra, which should help clarify the nature of algebraic thinking at the elementary level in the CCSSM. The paragraph below describes Heeffer's characterization of *nonsymbolic algebra* and *symbolic algebra*. Read it slowly and draw on your prior mathematical experiences to see whether the distinction between the two views of algebra makes sense to you.

> Let us call (nonsymbolic) algebra *an analytical problem-solving method for arithmetical problems in which an unknown quantity is represented by an abstract entity*. There are two crucial conditions in this definition: *analytical*, meaning that the problem is solved by considering some unknown magnitudes hypothetical and deductively deriving statements so that these unknowns can be expressed as a value, and an *abstract entity* that is used to represent the unknowns. This entity can be a symbol, a figure, or even a color .... More strictly, symbolic algebra is *an analytical problem-solving method for arithmetical and geometrical problems consisting of systematic manipulation of a symbolic representation of the problem*. Symbolic algebra thus starts from a symbolic representation of a problem, meaning something more than a shorthand notation.

One easy way of thinking about the two views is to consider CCSSM practice standard 2, *reasoning abstractly and quantitatively*, which is another way of interpreting symbolic and nonsymbolic algebraic approaches to solving mathematical problems. Practice standard 2 emphasizes both aspects of contextualizing and decontextualizing in problem solving activity. Applied to arithmetical problem solving, contextualizing and nonsymbolic algebra map well together since entities (i.e., whole numbers) and relationships emerge in the context of arithmetical problems and that the various operations and manipulations are seen as applications of certain arithmetical processes. Decontextualizing and nonsymbolic algebra also map well together in which case students attend to the analytical methods that enable them to *manipulate the representing symbols as if they have a life of their own, without necessarily attending to their referents.* In the following statement below, also taken from Practice Standard 2, think of numbers and their units as representing abstract entities and the relevant calculations and properties of operations and objects that are used to manipulate the entities as the analytical method. From the description, the initial phase in quantitative reasoning is appropriately nonsymbolic algebraic in character, as follows:

> Quantitative reasoning entails habits of creating a coherent representation of the problem at hand; considering the units involved; attending to the meaning of quantities, not just how to compute them; and knowing and flexibly using different properties of operations and objects.

Hence, arithmetical problem solving is not just a simple matter of combining whole numbers since the underlying processes are nonsymbolic-algebraic in context. Any instruction that simply takes a *nonalgebraic* approach to problem solving is most likely going to produce students who can only demonstrate rote learning and problem spotting.

For example, problem solving situations that ask them to basically apply steps in a procedure without helping them understand the underlying algebraic structures will most likely develop a view in which arithmetic and algebra are two separate and distinct subjects. Another example is illustrated in the two contrasting responses below from two fictitious first-grade students named Peter and Elizabeth. The two responses capture common and daily occurrences of thinking among young children who are learning to add two numbers that sum to 20 for the first time. Peter relied heavily on the blocks to count and engage in a counting-all action. Unfortunately, the nonalgebraic character of his thinking prevented him from seeing meaningful analytical relationships across the two tasks. Elizabeth's nonsymbolic algebraic approach enabled her to reason in a more efficient and sophisticated manner. She demonstrated analytical subitizing when she quickly decomposed the two-digit numbers in terms of tens and ones. She also understood the value of counting on from the larger number, enabling her to manage her calculations well. In her counting-on action, she modeled the commutative property for addition. More formally, Elizabeth demonstrated a deductively-driven analytical method of counting, unlike Peter who engaged in a nonalgebraic arithmetical way of counting, that is, he was simply doing arithmetic.

Teacher: *Show me how to find the sum of 11 and 12.*

Peter, first grade student, gathers a pile of 11 blocks and another pile of 12 blocks.

Peter: *1, 2, 3, 4, 5, 6, 7, 8, 9, 10, 11. There are 11 blocks here. 1, 2, 3, 4, 5, 6, 7, 8, 9, 10, 11, 12. There are 12 blocks here. So 1, 2, 3, 4, 5, 6, 7,*

> *8, 9, 10, 11, 12, 13, 14, 15, 16, 17, 18, 19, 20, 21, 22, 23. There are 23 blocks.*

Teacher:	*Good job, Peter. Do we have other ways of finding the sum?*

Elizabeth raises her hand and offers another suggestion.

Elizabeth:	*I know that 11 is 1 ten and 1 one and that 12 is 1 ten and 2 ones. So that's 2 tens, 10, 20, and I put 20 in my head and put 2 and 1 on my fingers. So 20, 21, 22, 23.*
Teacher:	*Good job, Elizabeth. How about finding the sum of 11 and 3?*
Peter:	*1, 2, 3, 4, 5, 6, 7, 8, 9, 10, 11. Then 1, 2, 3. So, 1, 2, 3, 4, 5, 6, 7, 8, 9, 10, 11, 12, 13, 14. The sum is 14.*
Elizabeth:	*Oh that's easy. You have 1 ten, so 10, then add 3 more and 1 more. So 10 in my head, 11, 12, 13, 14.*

Teaching to the CCSSM means that all students need algebra to do arithmetic, a view that fits nicely with Heeffer's point about the role of "deductively deriving statements" in solving mathematical problems. Otherwise, every problem is a new problem as Peter and many other young children tend to demonstrate in mathematical activity. Algebra is not something that you simply impose from the outside like ornaments on a Christmas tree. Meaningful arithmetical activity needs to be *nonsymbolic-algebraic* at the very least in order to help to help students avoid the gap trap, which sees arithmetic and algebraic as two different types of mathematical activity.

If algebraic thinking at the elementary level uses numbers as entities and not variables, which is how adults often perceive algebra, then how does thinking in variables emerge in arithmetical activity at the elementary level? There are two responses to this question. The first response involves helping students perceive numbers as *quasi-variables*. The second response involves having them shift their attention towards the *general power of a method*, which some scholars view in terms of *schemes*, that is, patterns of stable action. Other scholars prefer to call it *structure*. Both terms can be used interchangeably for the time being.

Heeffer notes that among Babylonian (and Arabic) mathematicians, the absence of variables in the way they processed arithmetical problems did not deter them from grasping the abstract nature of the unknowns and the analytic procedures that they used to solve the problems. While their solutions to problems primarily employed numbers, they, in fact, used them to convey how they actually perceived the generality of the corresponding methods of computation that applied to all problems belonging to the same category. Such numbers play the role of *quasi-variables*. The following examples illustrate how quasi-variables are used in the context of Practice Standard 8, looking for and expressing regularity in repeated reasoning, to convey deductively-drawn algebraic structures:

First-grade students who claim that $7 + 8 = 8 + 7 = 15$, $2 + 4 = 4 + 2 = 6$, and $5 + 4 = 4 + 5 = 9$, ... implicitly understand the general meaning of the commutative property for addition (**1.OA.3**).

Second-grade students who claim whole numbers whose ones digits are 0, 2, 4, 6, and 8 have the same visual representations (i.e., pairs of dots) understand the even parity concept of number (**2.OA.3**).

Third-grade students who think that $4 = 2 + 2$, $8 = 4 + 4$, and $20 = 10 + 10$ understand the claim that any multiple of 4 can always be decomposed into two equal addends (**3.OA.9**).

In some cases, visual diagrams are used to represent variables as unknowns. For example, the US-adopted Singapore texts consistently employ bar diagrams in arithmetical problem solving as visual placeholders for (letter) variables. Such diagrams often emerge as schemes. For example, the multiplication compare problem shown in Figure 5.1 has been solved using a bar diagram model (3.OA.3).

A blue marble costs $5. A red marble costs 4 times as much as the blue marble. How much does the red marble cost? (Or: A rubber band is 5 cm long. How long will the rubber band be when it is stretched to be 4 times as long?)

Solution: (Processing Phase)

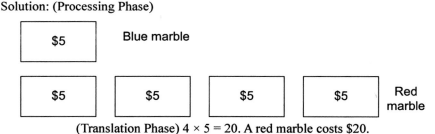

(Translation Phase) $4 \times 5 = 20$. A red marble costs $20.

Figure 5.1. A visual analysis involving a multiplication compare problem in third grade

a. Work with a pair and solve the remaining two multiplication compare problems in Table 2 of the CCSSM on p. 89 using bars. When you are done, assess how solving problems with bar diagrams accentuate the nonsymbolic-algebraic character of such problems that belong to the same category (i.e., they are all multiplication compare problems).

Various pattern generalization tasks such as the *Building a Hexagon Flower Garden Design* in section 2.3 provide another instance of nonsymbolic algebra. Fifth-grade students learn to abduce – that is, to *look for and make use of structures* (Practice Standard 7) – and induce – that is, *to express regularity in repeated reasoning* (Practice Standard 8), two practice standards that reflect core processes in the construction of a generalization in mathematics. They are nonsymbolic because the structures and generalizations that emerge are still linked to the relevant contexts. For example, the generalizations offered by Ava, Bert, and Ces in relation to the pattern shown in Figure 2.2 have been drawn from the assumptions employed in that particular activity. In section 5.5, you will deal with pattern generalization from both nonsymbolic and symbolic algebraic contexts.

All arithmetical problems in the elementary mathematics curriculum require students to manipulate numbers, perform operations, and establish general mathematical relationships in a decontextualized activity. These problems provide them with an opportunity to experience the symbolic algebraic nature of arithmetical activity early in their learning. For example, some third-grade students experience considerable difficulty in committing to memory the multiplication table involving factors 6 through 9. In such cases, they learn to decompose factors into more familiar factors (e.g., $7 \times 7 = (7 \times 5) + (7 \times 2) = 35 + 14 = 49$). Thus, symbolic algebra becomes a tool for *manipulating the representing symbols as if they have a life of their own, without necessarily attending to their referents* (Practice Standard 2).

Suffice it to say, teaching and learning operations, equivalent relationships, and patterns at the analytical elementary level involve conceptualizing the relevant abstract entities and analytical processes in an algebraic context. If you investigate the clusters of content standards in the OA domain carefully, they address the following concepts and processes below, which, as a matter of fact, characterize the big ideas in symbolic algebra in middle school and high school.

- (K–5) Implementing the four fundamental operations as general methods for combining and generating whole numbers;
- (K–5) Forming equivalent expressions;
- (1–5) Understanding the general meaning of the equal sign;
- (1–5) Inferring solutions of arithmetical problems within the same category or type in a general way; solutions involving arithmetical problems in a general way;
- (3–5) Pattern generalizing as instantiating nonsymbolic and symbolic algebraic structures

Hence, all fundamental and important algebraic concepts and processes in Algebra 1 and beyond reflect, in the words of Colin Maclaurin, a famous mathematician, "operations and rules similar to those in common arithmetic, founded upon the same principles." Teaching arithmetic to elementary school students should, thus, strive to help them view and employ nonsymbolic algebra in concrete contexts.

5.2 THE FOUR FUNDAMENTAL OPERATIONS AS GENERAL METHODS FOR COMBINING AND GENERATING MORE NUMBERS

5.2.1 Addition

Explore the K through Grade 5 OA addition standards by addressing each task below.

a. What does it mean to add two or more numbers at the K and Grade 1 levels (**K.OA.1**, **1.OA.1**, **1.OA.2**, and **2.OA.1**)? What approaches will help students understand the different meanings of addition?

b. There are two order properties for addition, namely, the commutative and associative properties (**1.OA.3**). The following three examples below demonstrate the commutative property.

$$2 + 5 = 5 + 2 = 7 \qquad 9 + 3 = 3 + 9 = 12 \qquad 4 + 11 = 11 + 4 = 15$$

The following three examples below demonstrate the associative property.

$$2 + 4 + 5 = (2 + 4) + 5 = 2 + (4 + 5) = 11$$
$$5 + 1 + 3 = (5 + 1) + 3 = 5 + (1 + 3) = 9$$
$$12 + 2 + 4 = (12 + 2) + 4 = 12 + (2 + 4) = 18$$

Both represent two different meanings of order. Carefully explain the difference between the two properties.

c. Obtain the sum of each expression below.

$$5 + 3 = \underline{\quad} \qquad 4 + 2 = \underline{\quad} \qquad 3 + 4 = \underline{\quad} \qquad 5 + 8 = \underline{\quad} \qquad 9 + 10 = \underline{\quad}$$

When you work with first-grade students, some of them will most likely use a counting all strategy to obtain the sums. A more effective strategy involves counting on (**1.OA.5**) beginning with the larger number. For example, in the case of $5 + 8$, a first-grade student will say, "8 in my head, so 8. Now using my 5 fingers, 9, 10, 11, 12, 13. So $5 + 8$ equals 13." What makes this particular addition strategy scheme effective? Also, what is the significance of knowing the commutative property in these cases?

d. How might you use a counting on strategy to help first-grade students solve for the unknown value in each incomplete number sentence (or number equation) below (**1.OA.8**)?

$$8 + \underline{\quad} = 11 \qquad \underline{\quad} + 6 = 7 \qquad 3 + \underline{\quad} = 12 \qquad \underline{\quad} + 9 = 17$$

e. First-grade students can add numbers that involve regrouping. (They formally deal with regrouping in second grade.) Add the following pairs of numbers below.

$$11 + 9 = \underline{\quad} \qquad 5 + 12 = \underline{\quad} \qquad 3 + 13 = \underline{\quad} \qquad 16 + 4 = \underline{\quad}$$

What algebraic strategy supports such processing?

f. How might you help first-grade students add each set of 3 whole numbers below (**1.OA.2**) in a systematic manner? How might they reason mathematically so that their answers are well justified and valid?

$$5 + 3 + 6 = \underline{\quad} \qquad 3 + 4 + 7 = \underline{\quad} \qquad 4 + 11 + 3 = \underline{\quad}$$

5.2.2 Subtraction

Work with a pair to accomplish each task below.

a. What does it mean to subtract two whole numbers at the K and Grade 1 levels (**K.OA.1, 1.OA.1, 1.OA.4**, and **2.OA.1**)? What approaches will help them learn the different meanings of subtraction? How is the concept of subtraction related to the concept of addition?

b. How might you teach first-grade students to obtain the difference of each subtraction expression below by using their fingers? Which definition of subtraction matters?

$$4 - 2 = \underline{\quad} \qquad 9 - 5 = \underline{\quad} \qquad 8 - 1 = \underline{\quad}$$

c. The following subtraction problems represent appropriate first-grade problems that involve regrouping.

$$13 - 4 = \underline{\quad} \qquad 16 - 9 = \underline{\quad} \qquad 20 - 11 = \underline{\quad}$$

How might you teach them to use counting on as an alternative strategy (**1.OA.4**)? Discuss its advantages and disadvantages. Which definition of subtraction matters in this case?

5.2.3 Multiplication

Work with a pair and do the following tasks together.

a. Carefully explain each factor in the notation a x b = c, where a, b, and c are whole numbers (**3.OA.1**). What are some possible consequences if students are not careful and precise about the meaning of each factor? Learn the meanings of the following terms: multiplier, multiplicand, and product.

b. Several experts have noted that "multiplication simply is not repeated addition." Access the following link below for an argument essay by Keith Devlin, a mathematician.

http://www.maa.org/devlin/devlin_06_08.html.

When is multiplication repeated addition and when is it not repeated addition? Should this concern you as an elementary teacher? How is the concept of multiplication defined in third grade (**3.OA.1**)? How does that definition help students in fifth grade when they interpret the concept of multiplication in terms of scaling (**5.NF.5**)?

Illustrate visually whether a third-grade understanding of multiplication of whole numbers using an equal-group (set) model is sufficient in dealing with fourth- and fifth grade multiplicative expressions as $6 \times \frac{1}{3}$, $\frac{1}{3} \times 6$ (**4.NF.4, 5.NF.4,** and **5.NF.5**), $\frac{1}{3} \times \frac{1}{3}$, and $\frac{1}{3} \times \frac{5}{6}$ (**4.NF.4, 5, NF.4,** and **5.NF.5**).

c. Create a graphic organizer such as the one shown in Activity Sheet 2.3 that will help second-grade students understand the different meanings and representations of multiplication involving two whole numbers (**2.OA.4, 3.OA.1**, and **4.OA.1**). How significant is the experience of knowing different representations for visualizing multiplication of two whole numbers?

d. How does grouping a set of objects up to 20 by a pairing process help second-grade students determine the parity of the set (**2.OA.3**)?

e. Why do third-grade students need to learn the order properties for multiplication (**3.OA.5**)?

f. How can you use a rectangular array of objects to explain the meanings of factors and multiples in multiplication (**4.OA.4**)? Demonstrate by using a specific example.

g. How does knowing how to count by 2s, by 5s, by 10s, and by 100s in second grade (**2.OA.3** and **2.NBT.2**) prepare students to multiply in third grade?

h. By the end of third grade, students should have committed to memory all products of two one-digit numbers (**3.OA.7**). Find online resources that will help them achieve this standard. For example, the following links below in relation to counting by 2s teach students to memorize a sequence of products through singing.

> http://www.youtube.com/watch?v=8wwydguSKOU
> http://www.youtube.com/watch?v=hae10bsW_CM

The resources below use finger math and patterns to help them multiply single-digit whole numbers by 9.

> http://www.youtube.com/watch?v=AnsoxGqDOoo
> http://www.eduplace.com/math/mw/models/overview/3_9_2.html

Make sure you obtain resources for all factors from 1 to 10.

i. One strategy that can help some third-grade students obtain products involving "difficult" factors involves decomposing one of the factors in terms of two or more familiar factors. For example, to find the product of 6 × 7, first express 7 as 5 + 2 and then obtain the sum of 6 × 5 and 6 × 2. Discuss advantages and disadvantages of this strategy.

j. Assume that none of the strategies you listed in (h) are effective in helping third-grade students remember their multiplication table. Does that mean they are not ready and that you should allow them to skip this standard for later? What else can you do to help them learn their multiplication table?

k. Find online resources that can help you teach fourth-grade students the meanings of prime and composite numbers (**4.OA.4**). One concrete approach involves having them generate rectangles involving unit squares (i.e., squares with dimensions 1 unit by 1 unit) with areas that are equal to specific whole numbers. Consider the two examples below.

2 is prime.

4 is composite.

How do you process the above visual approach in class to help them construct their understanding of prime and composite numbers?

5.2.4 Division

Work with a pair and explore the following tasks below.

   a. Solve each *partitioning* problem below. Draw first and then write a number sentence.

      1. Divide 12 objects into 3 equal groups. How many objects are there in each group?

      2. Divide 18 objects into 9 equal groups. How many objects are there in each group?

   What strategy did you employ to solve each problem?

   Carefully explain each letter in the notation $c \div a = b$, where c, a, and b are whole numbers and a is not equal to 0. How is this division notation related to the multiplication notation $a \times b = c$ in section 5.2.3 item (a)? Learn the meanings of the following terms: dividend, divisor, and quotient. Explain the meaning of the term *partitioning* in the context of the above two (problems and carefully describe the units associated with each quantity. (**3.OA.2**).

   b. Solve each *measuring* problem below. Draw first and then write a number sentence for your answer.

      1. 12 is how many equal groups of 3?

      2. 45 is how many equal groups of 5?

   What strategy did you employ to solve each problem?

   Carefully explain each letter in the notation $c \div b = a$, where c, b, and a are whole numbers and b is not equal to 0. How is this division notation related to the multiplication notation $a \times b = c$ in section 5.2.3 item (a)? Explain the meaning of the term *measuring* in the context of the above two problems and carefully describe the units associated with each quantity. (**3.OA.2**).

   c. A certain story begins with the following statement: "I have $24." Complete the story by developing a division problem that conveys (1) partitioning and (2) measuring.

d. How can you use a rectangular array of objects to explain the concept of division as an unknown-factor problem (**3.OA.6**)? Demonstrate by using a specific example. What happens if you change the array model to an area model?

e. Division of whole numbers has also been defined as repeated subtraction. Illustrate with an example.

f. How does knowing the multiplication table help all third grade students solve division problems proficiently? Demonstrate by using a specific example.

g. Division with remainders is formally pursued in fourth grade (**4.OA.3**). Construct partitioning and measuring problems that involve remainders.

h. How many remainders are possible if a number is divided by:

(i) 2?   (ii) 3?   (iii) 4?   (iv) 5?   (v) n?

In each case, name the remainders.

i. Carefully define the following terms that are relevant to the concept of division divisible; divides; and multiples of. For example: 4 is divisible by 2; 2 divides 4; 4 is a multiple of 2; 7 is not divisible by 2; 2 does not divide 7; 7 is not a multiple of 2; 2 is not a multiple of 4.

j. Search online resources that will help you teach divisibility rules for: 2, 3, 4, ..., 10. Do fourth-grade students need to know them? Access the Smarter Balanced Assessment sample task called *The Contest* from the following link:http://sampleitems.smarterbalanced.org/itempreview/sbac/index.htm. Solve the task consisting of 4 items. What type of division problem does the task model? How does having some understanding of the divisibility rules help 4th-grade students deal with the task?

5.3 FORMING EQUIVALENT EXPRESSIONS AND UNDERSTANDING THE GENERAL MEANING OF THE EQUAL SIGN

Elementary students initially learn to associate the equal sign, =, with *result*, which is helpful when they need to translate their processing of the basic operations in symbolic form. For example, the following situations below model the "results" view of the equal sign.

$4 + 5 = 9$ $5 - 3 = 2$ $5 \times 4 = 20$ $16 \div 4 = 4$

Unfortunately, if they associate the equal sign narrowly in terms of *result*, it fails to make sense in the following two types of arithmetical situations. How so?

a. For each set of tasks below, fill in each blank with the correct number to complete the sentence.

I. $3 + 4 = \underline{\quad} + 5$ (First grade); $23 + 12 = \underline{\quad} + 5$ (second grade); $3 \times 4 = \underline{\quad} + 6$ (Third grade)

II. $14 = \underline{\quad} + 4$ (first grade); $\underline{\quad} + 7 = 97$ (second grade); $324 = 300 + \underline{\quad} +$ 4 (third grade)

Holding a narrow "results" view of the equal sign can be harmful in fourth grade and beyond when students begin to deal with combined operations such as the one shown below.

Simplify the following expression: $2 \times 4 + 6 - 2$.

For example, a significant number of students' written work has been shown to employ *incorrect continued equality*, which is a sloppy way of writing solutions in mathematics. Such careless work violates Practice Standard 6, *attending to precision*, since it depends on a narrow understanding of the equal sign as *result*. The written solution below illustrates a string of equal signs that incorrectly translates in symbolic form a rather correct arithmetical processing of expressions.

$$2 \times 4 = 8 + 6 = 14 - 2 = 12$$

Consequently, you will need to provide all elementary students with learning experiences that will enable them to develop a much broader sense of the equal sign. One such experience involves having them conceptualize the equal sign in terms of the relation *is the same as* or *equivalent*. For example, the use of the equal sign below relative to the task of finding all addition facts for the number 10 reinforces the meaning of *equivalent expressions*, that is, expressions that have the same value or name the same number when simplified. *Equivalence* is a core concept in mathematics and having this broad sense of the equal sign early in students' learning experiences will benefit them in the long term.

$$10 + 0 = 9 + 1 = 8 + 2 = 7 + 3 = 6 + 4 = 5 + 5 = 10$$

Certainly the initial meaning of the equal sign, *result*, can be integrated in this much larger view. In fact, the continued equality in the above example uses both meanings of the equal sign.

The above Type II arithmetical tasks illustrate examples that require students to interpret the meaning of the equal sign as *equivalent*. The equation $14 = \underline{\quad} + 4$ does not begin with an expression that needs to be simplified. First grade students who understand place value should be able to quickly infer that the equation conveys an equivalent relationship between the number 14 in standard form and its place value form consisting of 1 ten and 4 ones. The same type of thinking can be employed in the case of the other two problems. Work with a pair and address the following additional tasks below.

b. How are elementary students expected to learn their addition and subtraction facts?
c. Addition and subtraction are related to each other. Multiplication and division are also related to each other. How does the *math triangle* diagram below help first-through third-grade students learn to generate the correct subtraction facts for a given addition fact? Illustrate with an example appropriate for each

grade level. Can you use the same approach to help third grade students learn to generate the corresponding division facts for a given multiplication fact? Illustrate with an example.

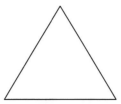

d. When students begin to use the equal sign, they need to learn to say the terms *equation* and *expression* correctly, which reflects proficiency in Practice Standard 6, *attending to precision*. Explain the meaning of each term. How come it does not make sense to say "simplify the equation $5 + 3 + 2$?"
e. What is the significance of using parentheses, brackets, or braces in writing and simplifying numerical expressions in fifth grade (**5.OA.1**)?
f. Trace the development of K through Grade 5 students' use and understanding of the equal sign in the CCSSM.

5.4 INSTANTIATING NONSYMBOLIC ALGEBRA THROUGH PROBLEM SOLVING IN ARITHMETICAL ACTIVITY

Work with a pair and do the following task below.

a. Consider your earlier experiences when you solved the two multiplication compare problems in 5.1(a) using a bar diagram approach. Which among the practice standards apply to word problem solving, and how so?

Meaningful problem solving experiences in arithmetical activity usually evolve in a nonsymbolic-algebraic manner, which supports the development of mathematical understanding. The CCSSM describes the hallmark of *mathematical understanding* in terms of students' ability to *justify, in a way appropriate to their mathematical maturity, why a particular mathematical statement is true or where a mathematical rule comes from.* For you, it means orchestrating nonsymbolic-algebraic learning situations that will help students develop appropriate and powerful schemes or structures in order to achieve mathematical understanding. No less.

Figure 5.2 shows a general problem-solving scheme and the associated representational scheme that you need to keep in mind when you engage in word problem-solving activity with your students. When they solve word problems, you should teach them to be mindful of the representations they use. In fact, you can only intervene and communicate with them at the representational level. Further, you learn something about their problem-solving scheme and are able to assess their level of proficiency by drawing on the representations that they share with you.

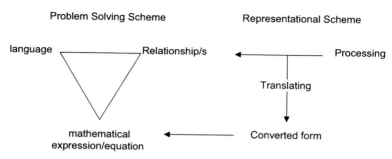

Figure 5.2. Word problem solving scheme and the associated representational scheme

The *problem-solving scheme* in Figure 5.2 uses the model of an inverted triangle to convey the idea that any mathematical expression or equation that is generated in word problem-solving activity represents a condensed or contracted recording of the initial processing phase. Hence, in word problem-solving activity, you need to be aware of the following two potential issues that elementary students may exhibit: (1) difficulty in processing; and (2) difficulty in translating. When you hear a teacher say, "My students can't solve word problems," it is necessary to know which representational component is causing the problem for the students. Especially with young children, the translation aspect often depends on their emerging understanding of notations and symbols. For example, if their dominant processing ability involves drawing pictures to solve problems, the converted mathematical form may or may not capture the correct relationships due to issues in the conversion phase (e.g.: wrong choice of numbers; incorrect counting of drawn pictures; incorrect use of signs).

Another pertinent issue in successful word problem solving at the elementary level involves the necessary mutual coordination between language and mathematical relationships. It is common practice among teachers to have children, especially English learners and students with mathematical difficulties, search for keywords as a method of contextual cueing in order to help them transition to the symbolic phase. However, that strategy alone is not effective in the long term and, especially, in complex cases of problem solving. Students who form incorrect mathematical expressions or equations because they rely solely on keywords alone exemplify rote or procedural learning without conceptual understanding. Consider the following problem below taken from Table 1 of the CCSSM on p. 88, which illustrates an addition/subtraction smaller unknown situation. Think about it for a minute.

Julie has three more apples than Lucy. Julie has five apples. How many apples does Lucy have?

Many first- and second-grade students who use keywords alone to solve word problems will most likely associate the term "more" with addition and quickly form the equation "5 + 3 = 8" without much thought. In this case, the initial dilemma clearly stems from their inability to process the correct mathematical relationship. The incorrect translation, in fact, captures an understanding of a different problem that also involves "more," which should be correct in that sense.

Work with a pair and do as follows.

a. Processing mathematical relationships in arithmetical activity can be accomplished in several different ways. In the preceding sections, you learned two powerful methods, namely, math triangles and bar diagrams. Both methods can, in fact, be used together. Demonstrate how this combined approach can be used to solve the four word problems in Tables 1 and 2 of the CCSSM (pp. 88-89).

b. Describe how word problem solving activity is expected to evolve in the CCSSM from K to through Grade 5. How do you see nonsymbolic algebra emerging in word problem-solving activity across the elementary grades?

5.5 PATTERN GENERALIZATION AS INSTANTIATIONS OF NONSYMBOLIC AND SYMBOLIC ALGEBRA

Patterns convey structures, and your first task in class is to emphasize the fact that they need to have well defined rules before any meaningful generalization can occur. Their feature, order, attribute, arrangement, or property should also be clear and precisely articulated so that students can easily tell whether an element belongs to the pattern. For example, students as early as second grade know that the numbers 2, 4, 6, 8, 10, 12, 14, 16, 18, 20, which emerge from counting by 2, are even because the visual representations in Figure 5.3 indicate a clear and consistent paired matching of circles across the instances (2.OA.3). The visual representations then become the basis for constructing well-defined rules that should enable them to infer that the whole numbers 22, 34, and 40 must also be even.

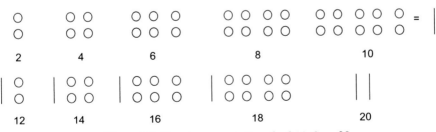

Figure 5.3. Visual representations for 2, 4, 6, ..., 20

In third grade, students further explore the consequences of such concepts and other number patterns that convey meaningful structural relationships. For example, Figure 5.4 illustrates arithmetical patterns involving even and odd sums. However,

2 + 4 = 6.	1 + 3 = 4.
4 + 8 = 12.	3 + 7 = 10.
4 + 12 = 16.	1 + 15 = 16.
The sum of two even numbers is even.	The sum of two odd numbers is even.

2 + 3 = 5.
4 + 9 = 13.
13 + 2 = 15.
17 + 4 = 21.

The sum of an even number and an odd number is an odd number.

Figure 5.4. Even and odd sums

the recommended level of explanation involves using properties of operations, which encourages them to begin to think in symbolic algebraic terms (**3.OA.9**). For example, while drawn circles can help them visually demonstrate the parity of sums involving particular pairs of whole numbers, the place value structure of whole numbers and the properties and operation of addition can be used to further help them understand why they only need to pay attention on the sums of the ones digits in order to determine the resulting parity. Work with a pair and do as follows.

a. Access the following link below.

http://www.illustrativemathematics.org/standards/k8

Open the Grade 3 link Operations and Algebraic Thinking. Click on the link that says "show all." Scroll down to 3.OA.9 and open the link that says, "see illustrations." Choose any one of the three tasks and solve it together.

In fourth grade, students generate number and shape patterns that follow a given rule. Further, they need to describe features or attributes in their patterns that are not readily apparent from the rules (**4.OA.5**). Work with a pair and do the following number patterns below.

b. Follow the same initial procedures in (a) above. Open Grade 4 link and access the tasks under 4.OA.5. Choose one of the two tasks and solve it together.

c. Look at the sums of three consecutive whole numbers shown below.

$$1 + 2 + 3 = 6$$
$$3 + 4 + 5 = 12$$
$$5 + 6 + 7 = 18$$
$$10 + 11 + 12 = 33$$

Find all the factors of 6, 12, 18, and 33 (**4.OA.4**). What factor is common to all four sums other than 1? Do the sums below share the same common factor? other than 1

$$13 + 14 + 15 = 42$$
$$30 + 31 + 32 = 93$$

Complete the following sentence: The sum of three consecutive numbers always _____.

How might fourth-grade students provide an appropriate explanation for their inferred generalization?

d. Consider the rule, *Add 5,* and begin with the number 2. Complete the following sequence of numbers below.

2, 7, 12, 17, 22, 27, ____, _____, _____, _____, _____

Why do the terms alternate between odd and even numbers?

Greco, 4th grader, claims that another rule for the above sequence is, "*2 plus 5 times the position number and take away 5,*" where position number refers to the numerical location of a term in the sequence. For example, the term 2 is in the first position, 7 is in the second position, 12 is in the third position, etc. Is he correct? Explain. If he is correct, what number corresponds to the 15th position? 20th position? 100th position?

Change the rule to *Add 4* and begin with the same number 2. Complete the sequence.

2, 6, 10, ____, ____, ____, ____, _____, _____, _____, _____

Establish a property that applies to all the terms in the above sequence. How do you know that the property is true for all the terms in the sequence?

Establish a direct rule for the new sequence similar to the one that Greco constructed for the sequence 2, 7, 12, 17, the term corresponding to the: 15th position; 28th position: 49th position; and 100th below.

Shape patterns in fourth-grade provide another interesting context that encourages students to explain the rules they construct relative to the sequences they generate. Further, shape patterning activity provides them with an opportunity to experience the significance of multiple representations such as ordered pairs and graphs on a coordinate plane, which they pursue in fifth grade (**5.OA.3**). Refer to Activity Sheet 2.3 for a sample of a graphic organizer showing four different representations for the Hexagon Flower Garden Design task, which exemplifies a shape pattern. Shape patterns can also be used to help students establish connections between and among different content standards. Work with a pair and accomplish the following two tasks below.

e. In Figure 5.5, 8 people can sit around one octagonal table. Sixteen people can be seated in the case of two separate octagonal tables. Twenty-four people can sit around 3 separate octagonal tables. And so on.

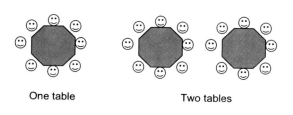

Number of separate tables	Total number of people that can sit around the tables
1	8
2	16
3	24
4	32
5	40

One table   Two tables

Figure 5.5. Separate octagonal tables pattern

(i) Marco, 5th grader, claims that to find the total number of people that can sit in any number separate tables, *keep adding 8*. Is he correct, and why?

(ii) Tony, Marco's classmate, says, *"The numbers are like the times table for 8."* Is he correct, and why?

(iii) Marina, Tony's classmate, says, *"Oh, I see twice the times table for 4."* How is she thinking about the terms?

(iv) James, Marina's classmate, claims that he sees another sequence that can describe the terms in the given pattern. How might he be thinking about it?

(v) How many people can sit around 234 separate octagonal tables? What concepts and processes are relevant in dealing with this particular task?

(vi) How many separate tables are needed to sit 1704 people? 310 people? What concepts and processes are relevant in dealing with this particular task?

f. In Figure 5.6, stage 1 has a cross shape figure that consists of 5 squares. In stage 2, one square is added on each side of the cross. In stage 3, the same action of adding 1 square of each side of the cross is performed. So, the rule *Add 4* means adding one square on each side of the growing cross pattern.

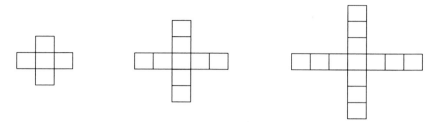

Figure 5.6. Growing Cross Pattern

(i)   Generate a fourfold graphic organizer similar to the one shown in Activity Sheet 2.3.

(ii) Carla, 4ᵗʰ grader, thinks that the recursive rule, *Add 4,* is not practical to use in case the problem involves figuring out rather quickly the total number of squares in stage 25. Do you agree, and why? What operation is involved in the recursive rule?

(iii) Devin, Carla's classmate, then suggests the direct rule, *"Add 4 groups of the stage number and then add 1."* How is he thinking about his rule? What operations are involved in his direct rule?

(iv) Rhina, Devin's classmate, says, *"Add 5 and 4 groups of the stage number and then take away 4."* Is she correct, and why? What operations are involved in her direct rule?

(v)   Jae, Rhina's classmate, say, *"I'm looking at my table and the numbers look like times 4 plus 1 to me."* Is she correct, and why?

(vi) It seems like direct rules are more efficient to use than recursive rules. Discuss advantages and disadvantages of each kind of rule.

g. The generalizations offered by Marina and Rhina convey one interesting way of thinking about standards **5.OA.1** to **5.OA.3**. Read the standards and explain how so. Then use their method to obtain direct expressions for each number pattern below with the identified recursive rule as a starting point. Explain your answer.

(i)   Add 2: 3, 5, 7, 9, 11, 13, 15, 17, …
(ii) Add 5: 7, 12, 17, 22, 27, 32, 37, …
(iii) Add 3: 2, 5, 8, 11, 14, 17, 20, 23, …
(iv) Add 4: 2, 6, 10, 14, 18, 22, 26, 30, …

For each pattern, form ordered pairs and graph them on a coordinate plane. Explain the meaning of each component in your ordered pairs. Connect the points and describe what you see.

Why are such sequences called linear patterns?

h. Use what you learn from task (g) to obtain a direct expression for each shape pattern below. Also, find a way to explain why and how each number in your direct expression makes sense relative to the pattern. Finally, determine the term corresponding to the: 12th stage; 25th stage; 100th stage; and 2455th stage.

(i) Add 5:

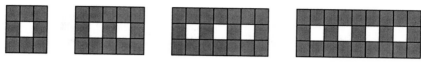

(ii) Add 4 in the case of the unshaded square tiles:

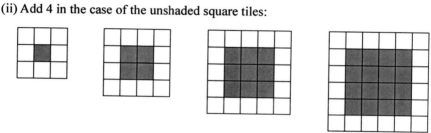

5.6 MAPPING THE CONTENT STANDARDS WITH THE PRACTICE STANDARDS

Work with a pair to accomplish the following two tasks below.

a. Use the checklist you developed in Table 2.3 to map each content standard under the *OAT* domain with the appropriate practice standards and NRC proficiency strands. Make a structure similar to the one shown in Table 3.2 to organize and record your responses.

5.7 DEVELOPING A CONTENT STANDARD PROGRESSION TABLE FOR THE OPERATIONS AND ALGEBRAIC THINKING DOMAIN

Continue working on the table that you constructed in section 4.7 to develop a nine-month progression of content standards under the *OAT* domain. Add the appropriate number of rows corresponding to the *OAT* domain standards. Then carefully plan a reasonable content path or trajectory for each standard over the indicated timeline. Remember that your table at this stage should reflect a reasonably tight mapping of interrelationships between and among the different content standard progressions involving both the *OAT* and *NBT* Part I domains.

CHAPTER 6

NUMBERS AND OPERATIONS IN BASE TEN (PART II)

In this chapter, you will deal with content-practice, teaching, and learning issues relevant to the four arithmetical operations of addition, subtraction, multiplication, and division involving whole numbers greater than 10 and decimal numbers up to the hundredths place. These content standards comprise the second part of the *Numbers and Operations in Base Ten* (NBT) domain from Grades 1 through 5 of the CCSSM. Table 6.1 lists the appropriate pages for your convenience. In this chapter, you will learn various mental, visual, nonvisual, standard, and nonstandard strategies for combining such numbers and the central role of base-10 place value structures in the development of such strategies.

Table 6.1. CCSSM Pages for the NBT Domain

Grade Level Domain	Standards	Page Numbers in the CCSSM
1.NBT	1 to 6	15–16
2.NBT	1 to 4	19
3.NBT	1 to 3	24
4.NBT	1 to 6	29–30
5.NBT	1 to 7	35

6.1 ANALYTICAL SUBITIZING IN KINDERGARTEN AND STICKS AND CIRCLES
OR LABELED CIRCLES IN GRADE 1

Content standard **K.NBT.1** is a foundational standard. Elementary students who do not demonstrate mathematical proficiency in analytical subitizing to 19 in terms of tens and ones by the end of kindergarten will experience considerable difficulty in the upper grades when they deal with problems and operations involving larger whole numbers. Instruction on numbers needs to make this happen for every K student. Activities that encourage them to group by tens and ones should help build this analytical subitizing foundation. Analytical subitizing is a nonnegotiable condition for further learning in upper-level school mathematics.

When K students move on to first grade, they continue to learn analytical subitizing through explorations involving tens and ones with the Dienes blocks. But you need to see to it that they are able to *psychologically distance* themselves from such manipulatives by scaffolding them toward the intended conceptual meanings. When they fail to come to terms with the underlying meanings, they will become

67

dependent on the blocks to help them count. Also in first grade, when students begin to draw longs for tens and squares for ones to represent two-digit whole numbers, many of them will take their time to draw neat squares, distracting some of them from learning more important matters about whole numbers and their structures. When that happens, their counting process tends to revert to a counting all strategy since they become wedded to the idea of drawing the correct number of squares for each long that they draw. As a recommendation, you need to negotiate with them a less detailed model for representing and counting by tens and ones than the model provided by the Dienes blocks. Figure 2.4 shows Fuson's sticks and circles and Singapore's labeled circles that can help first grade students shift their attention from pictures of longs and ones to diagrams (or, in Fuson's terms, *math drawings*) that symbolize the power-of-10 place value structure of numbers in a simple and direct manner.

a. Work with a pair and search online for other possible visual models of whole numbers and their structures. Which model appeals to you the most, and why?

6.2 ADDING WHOLE NUMBERS IN BASE TEN FROM GRADES 1 TO 4

When first grade students learn to analytically subitize by tens and ones proficiently, they also learn to decompose whole numbers in order, by tens first and ones next. Consequently, when they add pairs of numbers such as the ones shown below, the tens-and-ones structure cues them to add from *left to right*, that is, from the larger quantity to the smaller quantity, which should be strongly supported. Remember that their initial K experiences in exact number processing involve learning to count in multiples of 10 (**K.CC.1**), which can further explain the left-to-right bias. Many of them will also be drawn to processing the tasks verbally in which case you need to pay attention to how they record and write their sums. Others will need to draw tens and ones in which case you need to see to it that their visual processing helps them obtain correct translations in mathematical form (**1.NBT.4**).

$$21 + 34 = \underline{\hspace{1cm}} \qquad 15 + 23 = \underline{\hspace{1cm}}$$
$$\text{Eleven} + 7 = \underline{\hspace{1cm}} \qquad \text{Twenty-eight plus forty-one} = \underline{\hspace{1cm}}$$

When K and first-grade students have a strong visual grounding in tens and ones, that should enable them to handle simple addition with regrouping rather easily. For example, in Figure 6.1, the addition task $14 + 27$ necessitates *regrouping to form a 10* or, simply, *composing a ten* in the case of the ones digits (**1.NBT.4**).

Observe that the visual and verbal processing of addition in Figure 6.1 can also effectively scaffold the transition and translation to the mathematical form, which can then be used to explain why the standard algorithm for addition proceeds from *right to left*. *Standard algorithms* are explicit and translated recordings of deductively-closed processes that are rooted in some conceptual structure. Teaching them as

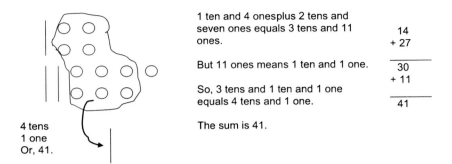

1 ten and 4 onesplus 2 tens and
seven ones equals 3 tens and 11
ones.

But 11 ones means 1 ten and 1 one.

So, 3 tens and 1 ten and 1 one
equals 4 tens and 1 one.

The sum is 41.

```
   14
 + 27
 ─────
   30
 + 11
 ─────
   41
```

Figure 6.1. Adding from left to right in first grade

mere procedures to follow is a terrible misconception that should not be shared with beginning learners. If they commit errors in performing an algorithm, having a firm grasp of the underlying conceptual structure(s) is the only way that can help them overcome such errors.

One consequence of the deductively-closed nature of the standard algorithm for adding numbers in second grade is the efficient manner in which students are able to deal with cases involving two or more two-digit addends (**2.NBT.5** and **2.NBT.6**). Figure 6.2 illustrates the further contraction of the nonstandard left-to-right addition into the standard right-to-left algorithm. Remember that standard algorithms are sophisticated, efficient, and shorter recordings of their initial nonstandard versions.

Figure 6.2 Nonstandard addition from left to right to the standard algorithm from right to left

Figure 6.3 is an example of an addition template that first- and second-grade students can use to help them make the transition from the visual to the numerical form. Certainly the template is unnecessary when addition tasks do not involve regrouping since they can simply add the numbers either from the left or from the right mentally.

Adding numbers from the left facilitates the development of mental strategies that are, in fact, useful everyday coping mechanisms. In classroom contexts, the strategy of using an *empty number line* provides an additional tool that can help students organize and record their addition processing. Figure 6.4 illustrates the two strategies in relation to the task of finding the sum of 14 and 27.

Hundreds	Tens	Ones	Add
			H ¦ T ¦ O +
			H ¦ T ¦ O +

Figure 6.3. Addition template

To add 14 and 27, I see 2 tens and 1 ten, which equals 3 tens, or 30. Then 30 + 7 gives me 37. Add 4 more, 37 in my head, 38, 39, 40, 41. So 14 + 27 = 41.

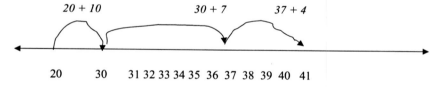

20   30   31 32 33 34 35 36 37 38 39 40   41

Figure 6.4. Mental and number line approaches for adding numbers

Many first-grade students find the activity of giving a two-digit number (1.NBT.5) difficult to accomplish. The source of difficulty is oftentimes not conceptual but linguistic. Using the base-10 visual structure for numbers can help them deal with this difficulty, especially when they are still in the process of acquiring competence in remembering number names. Figure 6.5 shows how this is accomplished. The linguistic difficulty is traced to students' inability to name the correct –*ty* name when the tens digits are added first, so thinking by tens first will facilitate the conversion to the appropriate linguistic convention.

Work with a pair and address the following issues below.

a. How does knowing the commutative property for addition property help first-grade students deal with problems involving adding two two-digit numbers or a two-digit number and a one-digit number? Explain.

What is 10 more than 34?

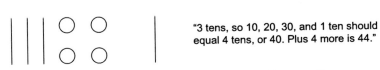

"3 tens, so 10, 20, 30, and 1 ten should equal 4 tens, or 40. Plus 4 more is 44."

Figure 6.5. Dealing with a 10-more problem visually

b. What is the significance of the associative property for addition in cases when second-grade students deal with adding up to four two-digit numbers (**2.NBT.6**)?

c. Should students be forced to choose between left-to-right and right-to left approaches for adding numbers? Many elementary teachers, in fact, believe that the sooner the kids learn to add from the right, the better the yield for them in the long term. What do you think, and why?

d. Many parents and elementary teachers believe that young children need to learn their procedures first before they begin to appreciate the underlying conceptual structures. In the case of addition, for example, they can learn to add two or more numbers expertly using the standard algorithm through extensive repetition and drill. What are the consequences of this particular teaching practice on students' learning of mathematics and their developing mathematical proficiency?

e. When elementary teachers claim that, "*My students don't know how to add their numbers,*" it needs to be seriously considered as a representational dilemma on two levels, namely, processing and translation. Finding out which level is problematic for an individual student can assist in decision making insofar as instruction and intervention matter. Discuss possible processing errors that first-grade students might exhibit in relation to adding numbers larger than 10. Discuss possible translation errors as well. What can you do to help them overcome or avoid such errors?

f. Each *NBT* domain from Grade 1 to Grade 4 addresses addition fluency using various strategies and algorithms based on place value structures and properties of addition. Identify the range of numbers that is appropriate for each grade level. How might you modify the addition template in Figure 6.3 to accommodate for larger whole numbers?

g. Choose a particular grade level beyond Grade 2. Construct an addition word problem and illustrate the addition process using the template you produced in item (f) above.

h. Search online for other popular mental or *informal* strategies for adding whole numbers. Use an appropriate mental/informal strategy to accomplish each textbook problem below.

Find the sum.
1. 24 + 6   2. 32 + 19   3. 258 + 12
4. Fill in the blank with the correct symbol (>, <, =): 16 + 34 _____ 19 + 21

i. Some teachers like routine knowledge such as the standard algorithm for adding whole numbers. Other teachers prefer adaptive knowledge such as those mental and informal strategies that you generated in (h) (refer to Figure 6.4 for an illustration). Discuss advantages and disadvantages of each knowledge type, and do you really need to choose?

j. What might you do in case you find yourself in a situation in which an elementary student is clearly demonstrating proficiency in adding numbers mentally or informally and is refusing to learn the standard algorithms?

k. For each problem in (h), first round the numbers to the nearest 10 and then obtain the sum. How do the estimated answers compare with the actual answers? What benefits do elementary students obtain from learning how to round numbers and estimate answers?

l. Search the internet for free online apps and games that pertain to the topics in this section games and assess potential benefits and possible concerns.

6.3 SUBTRACTING WHOLE NUMBERS IN BASE TEN FROM GRADES 1 TO 4

Subtracting two whole numbers without regrouping can be performed either *from left to right* or *from right to left*. Consider the following subtraction take-from or take-away problem below.

> *346 apples were on the van. A pie company came by and bought 125 apples. How many apples are on the van now?*

A bar diagram can be used to visually describe the situation, as follows.

Refer to Figure 6.6. Subtracting from the left, observe how the visual and verbal processing map well with the recorded numerical translation.

In the case of subtraction, students need to verify that their answers are correct through addition, which they can accomplish mentally from left to right. Notice the usefulness of the bar diagram in conveying the reasonableness of the corresponding check by addition. That is, when 125 and 221 are added together, the sum equals the original number of objects, 346. The bar diagram can also be used to explain why the answer to subtraction corresponds to the missing addend in the incomplete equation $125 + ? = 346$.

Work with a pair and address the following three questions below.

a. Identify counting strategies that can be used to obtain the result when 335 is subtracted from 648.

3 hundreds 4 tens 6 ones

1 hundred 2 tens 5 ones

_____

2 hundreds 2 tens 1 one

346
−125
_____
221

Figure 6.6. Subtracting two whole numbers from left to right

b. One alternative strategy that can be used to solve the subtraction problem in (a) involves counting on from the subtrahend to the minuend with or without the use of an empty number line. Try it.

c. Use the addition template shown in Figure 6.3 to develop a subtraction template that can accommodate whole numbers up to the hundred thousands place.

Subtracting two whole numbers with regrouping can also be accomplished from either *left to right* or *right to left*. Regrouping in subtraction fundamentally involves the action of *trading.* It should be noted that the popular notion of borrowing fulfills one aspect of regrouping action only, which explains why it is partially incorrect. Another way of thinking about regrouping action is to form equivalent groups in base 10 in order to support a take-away action.

Consider the following subtraction part-whole problem below. Draw a bar diagram that conveys your understanding of the problem.

In a room there are 458 children. 129 are girls. How many are boys?

Figure 6.7 shows two different solutions. In solution I, the subtraction process proceeds from the left, which means the difficult situation emerges in the last step. Consequently, students need to regroup by trading 1 ten for 10 ones and then subtracting 9 ones from 18 ones in the ones column. In solution II, the subtraction process proceeds from the right, which means the difficult situation emerges in the first step. Consequently, students need to regroup 5 tens and 8 ones into an equivalent group of 4 tens and 18 ones. Observe the central role of the visual diagram in conveying the underlying conceptual process involving subtraction with regrouping. The translated mathematical form emerges basically as a recording of the steps involved in the process. With repetition and deductive closure involving different combinations of whole numbers, students should be able to obtain two acceptable algorithms for subtraction. Solution II is the standard algorithm for subtraction, which favors right-to-left numerical processing.

Work with a pair and address the following issues below.

Solution I. Visual left-to-right processing

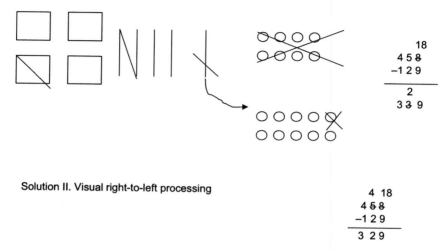

Solution II. Visual right-to-left processing

Figure 6.7. Subtracting with regrouping

d. Use visual and numerical methods to solve the following subtraction compare problem:

> Store A has 3000 apples. Store B has 2354 apples. How many more apples does Store A have than Store B?

Draw a bar diagram to help you establish a mathematical relationship. Then perform the subtraction process to obtain the answer to the problem.

A third method for subtracting two whole numbers involves counting on with or without the use of an empty number line. Illustrate one possible solution.

Which among the three methods do you prefer, and why?

e. What should you do if you have students who prefer to subtract visually than numerically?

f. Search online for other possible ways of performing subtraction with regrouping. If a method makes sense to you, does it work when you perform subtraction from either direction?

Second-grade students need to know how to perform regrouping action in subtraction in an efficient manner. Consider the subtraction problem shown in Figure 6.8. When they regroup, some of them tend to accomplish it in a procedural manner without reflectively thinking about the close link between the visual and numerical representations. Assume that subtraction proceeds from the right. Since

Find the difference: 45 – 29

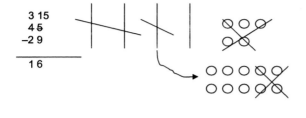

5–9 is not possible, so we need to regroup. Take 1 ten from 4 tens and trade 1 ten for 10 ones. Now there are 1, 2, 3, 4, …, 13, 14, 15 ones.

So now we can take away, 15 –9 = 6. 3 tens minus 2 tens is 1 ten.

The answer is 16.

Figure 6.8. Version i visual subtraction with regrouping

regrouping action is needed to carry out the subtraction process in the ones column, some of them who trade 1 ten for 10 ones tend to revert to a counting all action from 1 to 15.

One way to avoid the unnecessary reversal action is to deemphasize the trading action and reemphasize the fact that 4 tens and 5 ones and 3 tens and 15 ones are equivalent expressions, as shown in Figure 6.9. They can then employ a counting on strategy to obtain the two partial differences (i.e., 15 ones – 9 ones = 6 ones and 3 tens – 2 tens = 1 ten).

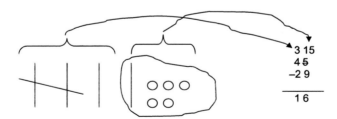

Figure 6.9. Version 2 visual subtraction with regrouping

Work with a pair and address the following issues below.

g. Develop Grade 4 word problems that illustrate each subtraction type below.

1. Take-from or take-away
2. Part-whole
3. Compare using the term *fewer*

75

Use visual and numerical methods to solve all three problems.

h. Assuming that first-grade students are proficient with visual and numerical methods for subtracting numbers, how might you help them deal with problems involving *10 less than a number* mentally without having to count (**1.NBT.5** and **1.NBT.6**)? Illustrate with an example. How might you help second-grade students to mentally subtract 10 or 100 from a given number from 100 to 900 (**2.NBT.8**)? How valuable are such experiences to first- and second-grade students?

6.4 MULTIPLYING WHOLE NUMBERS IN BASE TEN FROM GRADES 3 TO 5

Multiplying two whole numbers involves repeated addition. Figure 6.10 illustrates how visual processing and mathematical conversion can be coordinated to facilitate fourth-grade students' understanding of multiplication involving a 4-digit number by a single-digit number (**4.NBT.4** and **4.NBT.5**). Observe how the right-to-left numerical approach, which illustrates the *standard algorithm for multiplication*, makes sense from the point of view of convenience. That is, it is reasonable to start regrouping in base 10 from the right, where 10 ones become 1 ten, 10 tens becomes 1 hundred, 10 hundreds become 1 thousand, etc. Further, the product conveys a numerical recording of what remains under each column once all the required grouping actions are completed.

Another way of thinking about the standard algorithm is that it is a numerical contraction of a longer version. For instance, there are 12 ones under the ones column, which is equivalent to 1 ten and 2 ones. So the recording process is performed by leaving the 2 ones under the ones column and noting a 1 ten under the tens column. Under the tens column, there are 10 tens, which is equivalent to 1 hundred and 0 ten, so recording involves putting a 1 hundred under the hundreds column and a 0 ten under the tens column.

With numerical-based left-to-right multiplication, students need to calculate sums of *partial products*. For instance, the three numbers below the bar segment in Figure 6.10 convey three partial products that, when added together, produce the result of 702.

The area, array, or grid model in Figure 6.11 provides another visual structure for multiplying a multidigit number by a single digit number from any place. The same model can be extended to two multidigit factors, as illustrated in Figure 6.12.

Work with a pair and accomplish the following tasks below.

a. Carefully trace the development of the multiplication process involving whole numbers from third to fifth grade in the *NBT* domain of the CCSSM.

Why should third-grade students acquire proficiency in standard **3.NBT.3**?

b. Observe that the visual representation in Figure 6.10 shows 3×234. However, the numerical representation shows 234×3 in a vertical format. Why is that an acceptable practice?

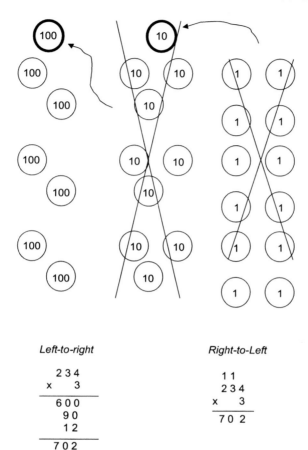

Left-to-right

```
  2 3 4
x     3
-------
  6 0 0
    9 0
    1 2
-------
  7 0 2
```

Right-to-Left

```
  1 1
  2 3 4
x     3
-------
  7 0 2
```

Figure 6.10. Multiplying 3 x 234 in fourth grade

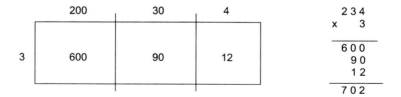

Figure 6.11. Area model for multiplication

Multiply: 234 x 321.

	200	30	4
300	60,000	9000	1200
20	4,000	600	80
1	200	30	4

```
  2 3 4        Standard
x 3 2 1        Algorithm
-------
6 0 0 0 0          1 1
  4 0 0 0        2 3 4
    2 0 0      x 3 2 1
  9 0 0 0      -------
    6 0 0        2 3 4
      3 0        4 6 8
  1 2 0 0        7 0 2
      8 0      -------
        4      7 5 1 1 4
-------
7 5 1 1 4
```

Figure 6.12. Area model for multiplication involving 2 multidigit numbers

c. The visual representations in Figures 6.11 and 6.12 illustrate the whole-number property called the *distributive property of multiplication over addition*. Explain how so.

d. Vina, a fourth-grade student, makes the following claim about multiplying multidigit numbers by a single-digit number: "*I think that we should simply multiply from the left in situations that do not involve regrouping.*" Is she correct? Illustrate.

Cheska, Vina's classmate, also makes a bold claim, as follows: "*It really doesn't matter where you start to multiply as long as there's no regrouping in any place.*" Is she also correct? Illustrate.

e. Many textbooks offer the *lattice method* to help fifth-grade students conveniently multiply two multi-digit whole numbers. Access the following link to learn how and why it works: http://youtu.be/Yt2atjULffY.

f. Use the lattice method to solve the following multiplication compare problem below. Draw a bar diagram first to help you set up a correct mathematical relationship.

A rubber band is 234 cm long. How long will the rubber band be when it is stretched to be 125 times as long?

Round the numbers appropriately to help you perform the multiplication process quickly. How reasonable is your estimate in comparison with the actual value?

g. Establish a pattern and state a generalization.

$2 \times 1 = 2$	$3 \times 2 = 6$	$15 \times 2 = 30$
$2 \times 10 = 20$	$3 \times 20 = 60$	$15 \times 20 = 300$
$2 \times 100 = 200$	$3 \times 200 = 600$	$15 \times 200 = 3000$
$2 \times 1000 = 2000$	$3 \times 2000 = 6000$	$15 \times 2000 = 30000$
$2 \times 10,000 = 20,000$	$3 \times 20,000 = 60,000$	$15 \times 20,000 = 300,000$
$20 \times 10 = 200$	$30 \times 200 = 6000$	$150 \times 2000 = 30,000$

Obtain the products below by drawing on your inferred generalization.

1. 3400×2 2. 4000×700 3. 213000×200

What is the significance of this patterning task on fifth-grade students' understanding of multiplying whole numbers by powers of 10?

h. Develop reasonable multiplication templates that will help students at each grade level establish a relationship between visual and numerical methods for multiplying whole numbers.

i. Search the internet for free online apps and games that deal with the topics in this section and assess potential benefits and possible concerns.

6.5 DIVIDING WHOLE NUMBERS IN BASE TEN FROM GRADES 3 TO 4

Every multiplication fact is related to two division facts. For example, the multiplication fact $3 \times 4 = 12$ is related to $12 \div 4 = 3$ (a measuring problem) and $12 \div 3 = 4$ (a partitioning problem). Hence, to find the quotient in a division problem, third-grade students need to convert the corresponding division expression in multiplicative form (i.e., a multiplication expression), which partly explains why they need to learn to commit the multiplication table to memory because of its relative usefulness in dealing with division problems. So, when students think about a quotient, c, relative to the division situation in which a certain whole number, a, is divided by a counting number, b, that is, $a \div b = c$, they can view c as the unknown or missing factor that when multiplied to b, the known factor, yields a, the known product (**3.OA.6**). They also need to exercise care and demonstrate precise language in describing the units corresponding to the quotient.

The concept of division can also be interpreted visually. Figure 6.12 reinterprets the division problem $40 \div 5$ in terms of finding the missing dimension when both the area and one dimension of a rectangle are given. Here, of course, it is assumed that third grade students have a firm understanding of the concept of area of a rectangle. If that is not the case, then a rectangular array consisting of rows and columns of objects (say, squares) will suffice.

Dividing a whole number by a counting number with no remainder means that the dividend is (exactly) divisible by (or is a multiple of) the divisor (or factor). The

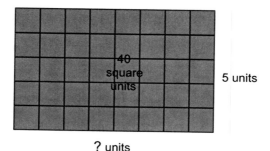

Figure 6.12. Division problem 40 ÷ 5 in terms of area-dimension relationship

situation with division becomes a bit complicated when remainders are involved, which students pursue in fourth grade. Relying on their expertise with the multiplication table and divisibility rules in fourth grade (**4.OA.4**), they should quickly see that the division problem 41 ÷ 5 involves a remainder of 1 when 41 is divided by 5 and that 41 is not divisible by 5. Further, when they record their answer, while it is reasonable to begin with the informal expression 8 *r* 1, they need to eventually express it in the correct format. They may use the *division algorithm* form, shown below,

$$41 = 5 \times 8 + 1 = 5 \cdot 8 + 1,$$

or they may use the alternative form involving fractions, as follows:

$$41 \div 5 = 8\frac{1}{5} \text{ or } 41 \div 5 = 8 + \frac{1}{5}.$$

The informal expression 8 r 1 is not a number even though everybody understands what it conveys. Practice Standard 6 requires students to *attend to precision* in the use of mathematical symbols, which explains the reference to the correct way of writing division sentences. Further, the fraction notation requires a firm understanding of fundamental concepts of improper fractions or mixed numbers, which students also learn in fourth grade (**4.NF.4a**). So timing and purpose matter. Overall, you need to see to it that they understand the meanings of notations as recorded translations of a visual or numerical process, including the possibility that such meanings may evolve over time, which is an acceptable mathematical practice.

Dividing a whole number by a counting number without regrouping and with no remainders can be performed from either *left to right* or *right to left*. Figure 6.13 illustrates the visual and numerical methods for teaching the topic to fourth grade students. In the example, dividing 336 by 3 can be interpreted as a sequence of three divisions. Proceeding from the left, 3 friends get 1 square, 1 stick, and 2 circles each. Of course the values matter (i.e., 300 ÷ 3 = 100; 30 ÷ 3 = 10; 6 ÷ 3 = 2). Also, the context (i.e., whether the division problem is partitioning or measuring) influences the manner in which grouping action is performed visually.

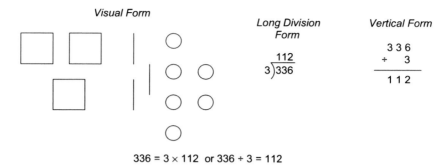

$$336 = 3 \times 112 \text{ or } 336 \div 3 = 112$$

Figure 6.13. Models for dividing 336 by 3

Some cases of division with regrouping and no remainders are rather complicated to accomplish with right-to-left processing. Figure 6.14 shows a simple division with regrouping problem that has been recorded in a modified long division format. Figure 6.15 shows a complex division with regrouping problem that has been recorded in a vertical format and in a textbook-based long division format that proceeds from the left, which represents the *standard algorithm for division*. When you teach division, you will need to draw on the corresponding visual processing model in order to emphasize the value of each digit in the dividend.

In Figure 6.14, the numbers in superscript form are the remainders. So, assuming a partitioning context and beginning from the left: 3 hundreds equal 3 groups of 1 hundred with no remainder; 4 tens equal 3 groups of 1 ten with a remainder of 1 ten; and 18 ones (regrouped) equals 3 groups of 6 ones with no remainder. Beginning from the right: 8 ones equal 3 groups of 2 ones with a remainder of 2 ones; 4 tens equal 3 groups of 1 ten with a remainder of 1 ten; 3 hundreds equal 3 groups of 1 hundred with no remainder; and the remaining 12 ones (regrouped) equal 3 groups of 4 ones. Either way, the quotient yields the same value.

Left-to-right

$$1 \quad 1 \quad 6$$
$$\overline{3 \,|\, 3 \,^0 4 \,^1 8}$$

Right-to-left

$$\begin{array}{l} 1 \quad 1 \quad 6 \\ 1 \quad 1 \quad 2 \end{array} \text{ Add 4 to 2}$$
$$\overline{3 \,|\, 3 \,^0 4 \,^1 8 \,^2}$$

Figure 6.14. Division involving simple regrouping using a modified long division format

In Figure 6.15, dividing from the left is easier to accomplish than dividing from the right. Assuming a partitioning context and beginning from the left, we proceed as follows: regroup the first two digits to form 10 hundreds, which equal 3 groups of 3 hundreds with a remainder of 1 hundred; regroup to form 10 tens, which equal

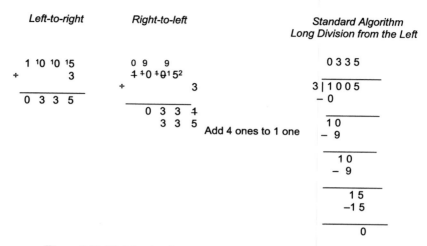

Figure 6.15. Division involving simple regrouping using vertical and long division formats

3 groups of 3 tens with a remainder of 1 ten; and regroup for the third time to form 15 ones, which equal 3 groups of 5 ones with no remainder. Beginning from the right: 5 ones equal 3 groups of 1 one with a remainder of 2 ones; regroup all the way to the thousands place by converting 1 thousand into 10 hundreds; regroup by decomposing 10 hundreds into 9 hundreds and 10 tens; regroup by decomposing 10 tens into 9 tens and 10 ones; 12 ones equal 3 groups of 4 ones and no remainder; 9 tens equal 3 groups of 3 tens and no remainder; and 9 hundreds equal 3 groups of 3 hundreds and no remainder.

Work with a pair and accomplish the following three tasks below.

a. Fourth-grader Marina makes the following claim about division of multidigit whole numbers by a single-digit counting number: *"I can perform division regardless of order in cases that do not involve regrouping."* What does she mean by that statement, and is she correct? Explain.

b. Make up a partitioning word problem involving a four-digit whole number dividend and a two-digit whole number divisor (**5.NBT.6**). Use both vertical and long division methods to solve the problem.

c Make up a measuring word problem involving a three-digit whole number dividend and a two-digit whole number divisor. Use the definition of division as repeated subtraction to solve the problem.

d. Search online for alternative methods or strategies involving division of multidigit whole numbers by a two-digit divisor and explain why they work.

e. Develop reasonable division templates that will help students at each grade level establish a relationship between the visual and numerical methods for dividing whole numbers.

f. Search the internet for free online apps and games that deal with the topics in this section and assess potential benefits and possible concerns.

6.6 ADDING, SUBTRACTING, MULTIPLYING, AND DIVIDING DECIMAL NUMBERS IN GRADE 5

Performing the four arithmetical operations involving decimal numbers to the hundredths place happens in fifth grade (**5.NBT.7**). The constraint regarding the kinds of decimal numbers that fifth-grade students pursue is reasonable, appropriate, and meaningful, especially when the context that is used to learn about them involves money and coins.

The addition and subtraction rules for whole numbers and decimal numbers to the hundredths place are the same. The only issue that you need to be concerned about is when students align decimal numbers in the same way they align whole numbers in a vertical format. For example, when students add 2.54 + 3.2, some of them will rewrite the numbers vertically in the following incorrect manner below.

$$
\begin{array}{r}
2.54 \\
+\ 3.2 \\
\hline
\end{array}
$$

One way to prevent that from happening is to include placeholder zeroes such as the one shown below.

$$
\begin{array}{r}
2.54 \\
+\ 3.20 \\
\hline
5.74
\end{array}
$$

Since students learn the relationship between fractions and decimals in fourth grade, you can further reinforce decimal addition and subtraction by manipulating the relevant decimal numbers as fractions. For example, the sum of 2.54 and 3.2 can be shown in two different ways. The first way stays at the level of decimal number representation. The second way involves initially converting the two decimal numbers into decimal fractions. When students perform the addition process, they should know how to add two fractions that have unlike denominators, which they also learn in fifth grade (**5.NF.1**).

$$
2.54 + 3.2 = \frac{254}{100} + \frac{32}{10} \cdot \frac{10}{10} = \frac{254}{100} + \frac{320}{100} = \frac{574}{100} = 5.74
$$

Work with a pair and do as follows:

a. Make up one addition put-together story problem that involves three decimal numbers as addends and regrouping. Use labeled circles to demonstrate the visual addition process.

b. Make up one subtraction take-apart story problem that involves decimal numbers and regrouping. Use labeled circles to demonstrate the visual subtraction process. Record your process in numerical form as well.

c. Given the following problem: *"Chuck has $20. He goes to a candy store and spends $3.65. How much does he have left?"* Solve this subtraction problem by employing a counting on strategy.

d. Construct addition and subtraction templates similar to Figure 6.3 with all the necessary components.

e. This particular task requires fractions. Find the sum or difference by first converting the decimal numbers below in fractional form. Then express your final answers in decimal number form.

(i) $21.35 + 7.15 + 9.02$ (ii) $16.5 - 7.25$

f. Rounding decimal numbers follows the same rules as rounding whole numbers. In the case of decimal numbers, rounding up or down can assist in performing the indicated operations in a convenient way. Estimate the sum and difference in each case below. Do all the relevant calculations mentally.

(i) $3.23 + 4.77$ (ii) $634.97 - 212.12$

The multiplication algorithm for decimal numbers up to the hundredths place follows the same structure for multiplying two whole numbers. However, students need to pay careful attention on the correct location of the decimal point in the final answer. One reasonable way of teaching the two operations without using fractions involves patterns in the place value structure of numbers (**5.NBT.2**), which students can easily verify by drawing on their everyday experiences with money.

For example, track a single-digit whole number, say, 2, each time it is multiplied by a power of 10. In Figure 6.16, the number 2 as a digit moves to the left when it is multiplied by increasing powers of 10 and moves to the right when it is multiplied by decreasing powers of 1/10. Thinking in terms of money, since 2 dimes have a total value of 0.20¢ and 2 pennies have a total value of 0.02¢, students should see rather easily that $2 \times 0.1 = 0.2$ and $2 \times 0.01 = 0.02$. Thinking in terms of patterns with the decimal point, it helps to view the number 2 in its decimal form 2.0 and that multiplying it by 0.1 moves the decimal point in 2.0 one place to the left and multiplying it by 0.01 moves the decimal point in 2.0 two places to the left. The experience is not totally new to students. For instance, they know that 2 $1 bills have a total value of $2 (i.e., no decimal point movement in 2.0), 2 $10 bills yield a value of $20 (i.e., move the decimal point in 2.0 one place to the right or, equivalently, move the number 2 to the left of 0 once), 2 $100 bills equal $200 (i.e., move the decimal point in 2.0 two places to the right), etc.

Extending the same patterning action to two decimal numbers, to obtain the product of, say 0.5×0.5, one possible mental strategy is to ignore the decimal points and multiply the corresponding whole numbers first, that is, $5 \times 5 = 25$, which is the same as 25.0. Then drawing on the findings from the preceding paragraph, move the

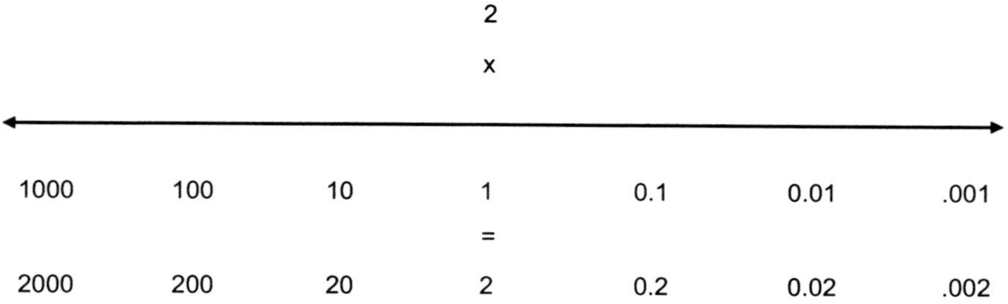

2

×

$$\longleftrightarrow$$

| 1000 | 100 | 10 | 1 | 0.1 | 0.01 | .001 |

=

| 2000 | 200 | 20 | 2 | 0.2 | 0.02 | .002 |

Figure 6.16. Tracking multiplication of 2 by powers of 10

decimal point in 25.0 twice to the left (why?). So, $0.5 \times 0.5 = 0.25$. Certainly, this particular mental strategy is even more interesting and conceptually enhanced once fraction multiplication is involved, as follows:

$$0.5 \times 0.5 = \frac{1}{2} \times \frac{1}{2} = \frac{1}{4} \times \frac{25}{25} = \frac{25}{100} = 0.25$$

$$\text{or, } 0.5 \times 0.5 = \frac{5}{10} \times \frac{5}{10} = \frac{25}{100} = 0.25.$$

When you teach the patterns involving decimal numbers up to the hundredths place, use "friendly numbers" in the beginning phase to help students enjoy and appreciate the underlying structures of the patterns. For example, have them quickly multiply the following decimal numbers below mentally first and then have them verify the results with a calculator.

0.25×3 2.25×0.1 $3.04 \times .02$ $15.2 \times .04$ $150.01 \times .05$

Work with a pair and do the following four tasks below.

g. Use labeled circles to find the product of 3×0.28. Then translate the visual process numerically by using a vertical format for multiplying numbers.

h. Construct a template with all the necessary components that will help students perform decimal number multiplication in an organized manner. Then use your template to multiply the following decimals fractions: 345.23×0.12; 54.32×0.7.

i. Multiplying two whole numbers involves repeated addition. How might you conceptualize multiplying two decimal numbers? Discuss situations in everyday life that justify the need to know decimal multiplication.

The division algorithm for decimal numbers up to the hundredths place follows the same structure for dividing two whole numbers with the additional condition that all divisors need to be in whole-number form to conveniently perform the division

85

process. From a psychological perspective, the conversion to a whole-number divisor should help fifth-grade students link the idea of dividing two decimal numbers with their earlier experiences of partitioning and measuring in division. For example, to obtain the quotient of $10 \div 2.5$, moving the decimal point in the divisor one place to the right also requires performing the same action in the dividend. So, $10 \div 2.5 = 100 \div 25$, which equals 4. Students can then verify that, indeed, $25 \times 4 = 100$ and $2.5 \times 4 = 10$. If they are fully proficient in fraction division (**5.NF.7b**), they can also transform the decimal numbers into decimal fractions and proceed as follows:

$$10 \div 2.5 = 10 \div \frac{25}{10} = 10 \div \frac{5}{2} = 10 \div \left(5 \times \frac{1}{2}\right) = 2 \div \frac{1}{2} = 4.$$

$$\text{Or, } 10 \div 2.5 = 10 \div \frac{25}{10} = \frac{100}{10} \div \frac{25}{10} = 100 \div 25 = 4.$$

One concern with content standard **5.NF.7** is that problems are supposed to be limited to division of unit fractions by whole numbers and whole numbers by unit fractions.

Figure 6.17 shows both vertical and long division formats relative to the division task, $2.368 \div 0.4$. First, move each decimal point one place to the right (why?). Then perform the usual division process. Interpreting the task in a partitioning context, consider a division problem that involves determining the amount that one person is expected to receive when \$23.68 is split evenly among four people. First, there is not enough 2 \$10 bills that can be shared equally among the four of them. There are, however, 23 \$1 bills that can do the task. After each friend receives 5 \$1 bills, three \$1 bills remain. Since \$1 = 10 dimes, a total of 36 dimes can be shared equally among them with each person receiving exactly 9 dimes. The remaining 8 nickels can also be shared equally among them. Hence, each person should receive 5 \$1 bills, 9 dimes, and 2 nickels or, \$5.92. Hence, $23.68 \div 4 = 2.36 \div 0.4 = 5.92$.

Long Division Form

```
        5 . 9 2
      _____
  4 | 2 3 . 6 8
    - 2 0
      _____
        3   6
      - 3   6
      _____
              8
            - 8
      _____
              0
```

Vertical Form

```
  2 3 . ³⁶ 8
  ÷         4
  _____
      5 . 9 2
```

Figure 6.17. Dividing $2.36 \div 0.4$

Work with a pair and do as follows:

j. Provide a visual representation that goes with the division process shown in Figure 6.17.

k. Divide 4.75 by 2.5. Interpret the task in the context of a measurement problem and explain each step in the division process.

l. Divide 0.35 by 12.5. What possible issues might occur when fifth-grade students perform the division process?

m. Construct a template with all the necessary components that will help students perform decimal number division in an organized manner. Generate two division problems and use your template to help you solve them.

n. While the rules for addition and subtraction of decimal numbers up to the hundrededths place are reasonable, the rules for multiplication and division seem to encourage procedural fluency over conceptual understanding. What kinds of teaching and learning might promote such a gap or dichotomy in students' thinking relative to these content standards, and how can they be prevented from occurring?

o. How does rounding decimal numbers support fifth-grade students' understanding of multiplication and division of decimal numbers? Provide examples to illustrate your claims and arguments.

p. Search the internet for free online apps and games that pertain to the topics in this section and assess potential benefits and possible concerns.

6.7 MAPPING THE CONTENT STANDARDS WITH THE PRACTICE STANDARDS

Work with a pair to accomplish the following task: Use the checklist you developed in Table 2.3 to map each content standard under the *NBT Part II* domain with the appropriate practice standards and NRC proficiency strands. Make a structure similar to the one shown in Table 3.2 to organize and record your responses.

6.8 DEVELOPING A CONTENT STANDARD PROGRESSION TABLE FOR THE OPERATIONS AND NUMBER THINKING PART II DOMAIN

Continue working on your domain table. First, add the appropriate number of rows corresponding to the *NBT Part II* domain standards. Then carefully plan a reasonable content trajectory for each standard over the indicated timeline. Also, keep in mind that your domain table at this stage is becoming more complex than before. Make sure that your table reflects a tight mapping of interrelationships between and among the different content standard progressions involving both the *OAT* and *NBT* domains.

NUMBERS AND OPERATIONS – FRACTIONS

In this chapter, you will deal with content-practice, teaching, and learning issues relevant to fractions and operations in the *Numbers and Operations –Fractions* (NF) domain from Grades 1 through 5 of the CCSSM. In particular, you will develop a teacher's perspective on their representations and the relevant core mathematical processes that depend on such representations. Table 7.1 lists the appropriate pages for your convenience. Notice the initial reference to several standards in the *Geometry* (G) domain. They ground first- through third-grade students' initial understanding of fractions in partitioning activities that involve having them divide whole shapes and unit segments into equal shares or parts. Labels of equal parts initially take the form of verbal descriptions (*half, two halves, thirds, two thirds, fourths, three fourths, three thirds, etc.*) in first and second grade, which support students' understanding of the numerical form $\frac{a}{b}$ in third grade when they conceptualize fractions as multiplicative expressions (i.e., as a multiples of $\frac{1}{b}$ units). The disembedding of a and b in $\frac{a}{b}$ as two whole-number units that are related by division emerges in fifth grade through equal sharing problems. In this chapter, it is both interesting and important to understand how an initial equal partitioning conception of fractions evolves into numbers as structured mathematical entities by the time students complete fifth grade CCSSM.

Table 7.1. CCSSM Pages for the NF Domain

Grade Level Domain	Standards	Page Numbers in the CCSSM
1.G	3	16
2.G	2 to 3	20
3.G	2	26
3.NF	1 to 3	24
4.NF	1 to 7	30–31
5.NF	1 to 7	36–37

7.1 EQUAL PARTITIONING OF WHOLE SHAPES IN HALVES
AND FOURTHS IN GRADE 1

First-grade students enjoy tasks that require them to thinker. To help them understand halves and fourths (**1.G.3**), they will need pairs of scissors, rulers, colored pencils, and patty paper sheets.

To introduce the notion of *halves*, have them trace a shape from the ones shown in Figure 7.1 on a patty paper sheet and cut along its perimeter with a pair of scissors. Then ask them to find different ways of folding the shape into two equal pieces and to use a ruler and a colored pencil to trace the crease formed by the fold. Once the crease is constructed, ask them to cut along the crease and verify that there are indeed two such congruent pieces. At this stage, it is reasonable for them to establish *congruence* informally by having them describe how both pieces are the same size and the same shape by moving the pieces around through actions of flipping, turning, or sliding. Finally, ask them to label each piece to help them remember the singular term, *half*. Discuss its plural form, *halves*, in class together. The translation from the verbal expression *half* to the numerical form $\frac{1}{2}$ takes place in third grade in the context of parts or shares that have the same area (**3.G.2**).

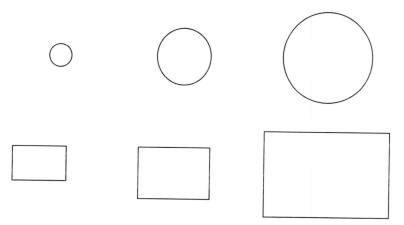

Figure 7.1. Small scale version of circles and rectangles

Repeat the folding-and-cutting process several more times using the rest of the shapes shown in Figure 7.1. Some students may choose not to cut along each crease to verify two congruent shapes. It is important, however, for them to know that a line of symmetry divides a whole piece into two congruent parts. Consistently ask them to label each part. Close the activity on halves by addressing the following questions together in class:

– *How do we make perfect halves?* (Show them large-scale copies of a circle and a rectangle.) *How do we obtain a half of this circle? A half of this rectangle?*
– *How can we describe this whole piece of circle in terms of halves and shares? How about this whole piece of rectangle?*

As an enrichment activity, Figure 7.2 shows different shapes other than circles and rectangles. Challenge them to divide each whole piece into two smaller congruent shapes.

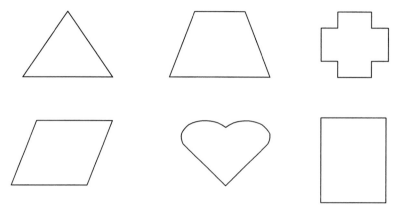

Figure 7.2. Small scale version of making halves

To learn about *fourths*, let them suggest different ways of partitioning a circle into 4 congruent parts. For each suggestion, pose the following question: *How do you know that you have 4 equal shares or 4 congruent parts?* Ask them to fold and cut to verify that their partitioning process is correct. Let them see that an easy way to construct four equal shares in a circle involves making two successive half folds, forming two creases that are perpendicular to each other. You may have to point out that the intersection of the two lines of symmetry coincides with the center of the circle. Give them time to label each part using the terms *fourth* and *quarter*. Emphasize the phrases *fourth of* and *quarter of*. Also, have them describe the circle in terms of fourths and quarters. Close the activity on fourths by addressing the following questions together in class:

– *How do we make perfect fourths?* (Show them large-scale copies of a circle and a rectangle.) *How do we obtain a quarter of this circle? A fourth of this rectangle?*
– *How can we describe this whole piece of circle in terms of fourths and shares? How about this whole piece of rectangle?*
– *Show 2 quarters. How about three fourths?*
– *(Show them copies of circles and rectangles with different shaded parts of halves and fourths.) Can you describe what you see in terms of halves and fourths?*

91

Work with a pair and do the following tasks below.

a. Find different ways of partitioning a rectangle into 4 congruent smaller pieces.
b. Halves can be used to make fourths. Use the same process to partition a circle into eight equal shares. (Note: Making eight equal shares is not a first-grade content requirement.)
c. Having first-grade student construct a *fourth* piece introduces them to *think multiplicatively* about fractions. How so?
d. Students learn the fraction notation $\frac{a}{b}$ in third grade (**3.G.2**). In first and second grade, there is an explicit emphasis on the verbal versions. Discuss potential benefits of this practice.

7.2 EQUAL PARTITIONING OF WHOLE SHAPES IN THIRDS AND CONSTRUCTING EQUIVALENT SHARES IN GRADE 2

In second grade, students continue to partition circles and rectangles into two and four equal parts. They also learn to partition into three equal shares and describe whole pieces in terms of 2 halves, 3 thirds, and 4 fourths (**2.G.3**). Figures 7.3 and 7.4 are additional activities that ask them to determine whether each indicated partitioning either by half or by fourth, respectively, is correct. Make patty paper sheets available for these two activities.

To partition a circle into three equal shares or *thirds*, ask them to first make a half fold (Figure 7.5a). Then ask them to fold the left (or the right) corner of the half folded piece over so that the edges are evenly aligned (Figure 7.5b). Have them fold the other corner over so that the final shape resembles a cone. Ask them to open the

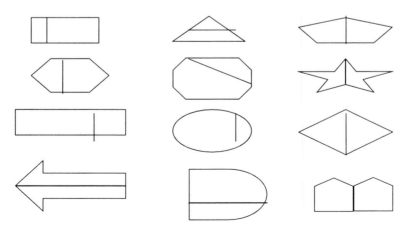

Figure 7.3. Which pictures show correct halves?

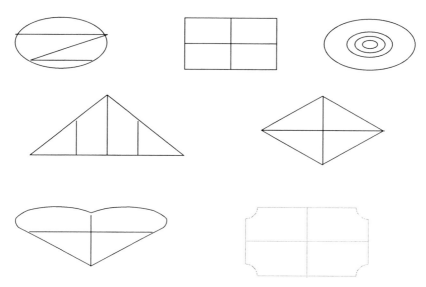

Figure 7.4. Which pictures show correct fourths?

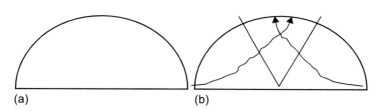

(a)   (b)

Figure 7.5. Partitioning a circle into thirds

trifolded half piece and cut along the two creases formed. Then have them open the three small shapes and verify that they are all congruent to each other. Ask them to label each shape and recompose to form a whole. Close the activity by addressing the following questions together in class:

– *How do we make perfect thirds from a whole circle piece?* (Show them a large-scale copy of a circle. Have them retrace the folding process. Do not cut but open the whole circle, which should show six equal parts. Have them point out the three segments that are needed to convey three equal shares on the circle.
– *How can we describe this whole piece of circle in terms of thirds and equal shares?*

Having students form halves, thirds, and fourths in a precise manner enables them infer a structure for constructing correct equal shares. Do not ask them to make rough sketches when it is easy for them to construct exact shares. Access the following site for additional information regarding four ways of folding a whole rectangle into thirds: http://www.wikihow.com/Fold-a-Paper-Into-Thirds.

As an enrichment activity, Figure 7.6 shows different shapes other than circles and rectangles. Challenge them to determine which ones show a correct partitioning into three equal shares.

Seeing equivalent parts drawn from identical wholes close second-grade students' explorations into fractions (**2.G.3**). They also establish equivalence visually, which can further support their developing analytical skills in figural combination and deconstruction. For instance, the two rectangles in Figure 7.7 are identical wholes with two equivalent versions of a fourth share. In establishing an equivalent relationship, some of them may start with the second figure and suggest moving and combining the four small shaded parts together so that they match the shaded part of the first figure. Others may just do the opposite and engage in deconstruction.

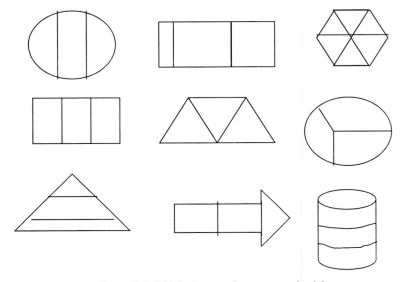

Figure 7.6. Which pictures show correct thirds?

Figure 7.7. Two equivalent versions of a fourth share

Work with a pair and accomplish the following tasks below.

a. Each set of figures in Figure 7.8 shows different shaded parts of the same whole piece. Which ones represent correct halves? Explain.

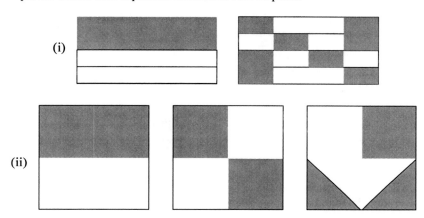

Figure 7.8. Equivalence tasks

7.3. UNIT FRACTIONS AND EQUIVALENT FRACTIONS WITH DENOMINATORS 2, 3, 4, 6, AND 8 AS EQUAL SHARES AND NUMBERS ON A NUMBER LINE AND WHOLE NUMBERS AS IMPROPER FRACTIONS IN GRADE 3

In third grade, students partition whole shapes into parts and shares that have equal areas. They also express parts and shares as unit fractions of their corresponding whole shapes (**3.G.2**). While the visual processing of fractions continues to draw on partitioning action, their translation skill shifts from the verbal to the numerical form. For example, verbal terms such as *half, third, fourth*, and their multiples such as *two thirds* and *three fourths* are converted to $\frac{1}{2}, \frac{1}{3}, \frac{1}{4}, \frac{2}{3}$, and $\frac{3}{4}$, respectively. The common unit, $\frac{1}{b}$, where b is a counting number, in fact, emerges as a unit fractional part of a whole shape and not as a separate relationship between a numerator and a denominator. Consequently, *proper fractions* of the form $\frac{a}{b}$, where a and b are whole numbers, $a < b$, and $b \neq 0$, are seen as multiplicative expressions, that is, $\frac{a}{b}$ represents a multiples of $\frac{1}{b}$, a copies of $\frac{1}{b}$, or a parts of size $\frac{1}{b}$ (**3.NF.1**).

Work with a pair and do the following tasks below. Assume knowledge of halves, thirds, and fourths.

a. Use circles and rectangles to construct 8 precise equal shares or congruent eighth parts. Provide a numerical label for each part.

b. When you partition a circle into three equal parts, as shown in Figure 7.5, you also construct sixths. How so?

c. Describe in multiplicative terms how fourths, sixths, and eights are related to either halves or thirds. Express your answers in numerical form.

d. Dave, a third-grade student, asks: "*Is a unit fraction a proper fraction?*" How might you respond to Dave's question?

In third grade, students begin to explore fractions as numbers on a number line diagram (**3.NF.2**), a one-dimensional representation of a whole piece (versus circles and rectangles that are classified as two-dimensional shapes because they have width and height). Work with a pair and do the following tasks below.

e. On a clean sheet of paper, draw an empty number line diagram. Locate two points on the line corresponding to 0 and 1. Label the points. Think of the interval from 0 to 1 as a whole unit (like circles and rectangles in the previous two sections) and call it a *unit segment*. Trace the unit segment on a patty paper sheet. Use the traced segment to construct halves, fourths, sixths, and eighths precisely on the number line diagram. Label appropriately and explain why halves, fourths, sixths, and eighths are called unit fractions on the number line (**3.NF.2a**).

f. Marian, Dave's classmate, raises the following concern: "*Are proper fractions points or lengths on a unit segment?*" How might you respond to Marian's question?

g. On a clean sheet of paper, draw five parallel unit segments. With or without the use of a patty paper sheet, construct two equal halves using the first segment. Locate the point $\frac{1}{2}$ on the segment. Express 1 in terms of a half. Can we express 0 in terms of a half, too? Label the three points appropriately.

Knowing where the point $\frac{1}{2}$ is located on the first segment, use the fact that $\frac{1}{4}$ is a multiplicative expression to trace all the fourths using the second segment. Carefully label all the fourths from left to right. Express 1 in terms of fourths.

Use the fact that $\frac{1}{8}$ is a multiplicative expression to construct and trace all the eighths Express 1 in terms of eighths the third unit segment. Carefully label all the eighths from left to right.

h. Use the fact that $\frac{1}{6}$ is a multiplicative expression to construct and trace all the sixths using the fourth unit segment. Carefully label all the sixths from left to right. Express 1 in terms of sixths. Which sixths correspond to the thirds? Use the sixths diagram to locate, construct, and label all the thirds using the fifth parallel segment.

i. How might you use the labeled diagrams you constructed in (g) and (h) to help third-grade students understand equivalent fractions (**3.NF.3**)? Which proper fractions are equivalent to $\frac{1}{2}$? $\frac{1}{4}$? $\frac{1}{3}$? 0? 1?

j. Compare the unit fractions $\frac{1}{2}, \frac{1}{3}, \frac{1}{4}, \frac{1}{6}, \frac{1}{8}$ assuming, of course, that all of them refer to the same whole **(3.NF.3d)**. Without having to draw, make a conjecture about the order relationship of all unit fractions relative to the same whole piece. Is a fifth smaller or bigger than a fourth? Is a seventh smaller or bigger than an eight? How does a tenth share compare with a ninth share and an eleventh share? What happens if we ignore the assumption of comparing unit fractions relative to the same whole piece?

k. *Improper fractions* are fractions of the form $\frac{a}{b}$, where a and b are whole numbers, $a \geq b$, and $b \neq 0$. Are all whole numbers proper or improper fractions **(3.NF.3c)**? Explain. Trace the development of students' conception of improper fractions in the CCSSM.

l. How might you use the visual representation of $\frac{1}{2}$ in Figure 7.9 to help third-grade students construct and establish the equivalent relationship $\frac{1}{2} = \frac{2}{4} = \frac{3}{6} = \frac{4}{8}$

(3.NF.3b)?

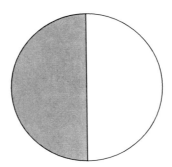

Figure 7.9. Shaded half of a circle

Can they use the same strategy to visually explain the relation $\frac{2}{3} = \frac{4}{6}$? Explain.

Figure 7.10 shows a picture of $\frac{1}{4}$. Visually establish the equivalence $\frac{1}{4} = \frac{2}{8} = \frac{4}{16}$.

m. How can third-grade students use the fact that $\frac{1}{8} < \frac{1}{6} < \frac{1}{4} < \frac{1}{2}$ to compare two nonunit proper fractions with the same numerator without having to draw them

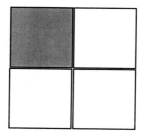

Figure 7.10. Shaded fourth of a Square

and assuming that they both refer to the same whole piece (**3.NF.3d**)? What happens if we ignore the assumption of comparing nonunit proper fractions relative to the same whole piece?

n. Complete the Fractions Puzzle activity in Figure 7.11. Discuss advantages and possible issues when it is implemented in class.

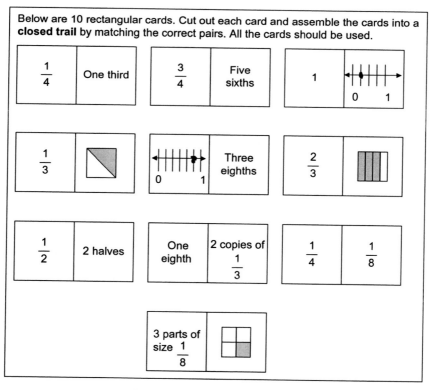

Figure 7.11. Fractions puzzle activity

o. Search the internet for free online apps and games that pertain to the topics in this section and assess potential benefits and possible concerns.

7.4 NUMERICAL EQUIVALENCE OF FRACTIONS INVOLVING DENOMINATORS 2, 3, 4, 5, 6, 8, 10, 12, AND 100, ALL IMPROPER FRACTIONS, FRACTION ADDITION AND SUBTRACTION WITH LIKE DENOMINATORS, SIMPLE FRACTION MULTIPLICATION, AND DECIMAL FRACTION ADDITION AND COMPARISON IN GRADE 4

Task l in section 7.3 provides a visual way of establishing and generating equivalent fractions. You can use it to show how and why multiplying both the numerator and denominator of a proper fraction by the same whole number produce equivalent proper fractions (**4.NF.1**). That is, $\dfrac{a}{b} = \dfrac{n \times a}{n \times b}$, where $b \neq 0$ and $n \neq 0$, n, a, and b are whole numbers.

For example, Figure 7.12 shows $\dfrac{3}{4} = \dfrac{3 \times 2}{4 \times 2} = \dfrac{6}{8} = \dfrac{3 \times 4}{4 \times 4} = \dfrac{12}{16}$. Students should see that because the same multiplicative action has been applied on all the equal shares of the fraction, it did not change the original value of the fraction. Further, multiplying a fraction by $\dfrac{n}{n}$, which equals 1, simply increases the number of equal shares.

  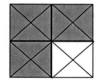

Figure 7.12. Visual processing for $\dfrac{3}{4} = \dfrac{3 \times 2}{4 \times 2} = \dfrac{6}{8} = \dfrac{3 \times 4}{3 \times 4} = \dfrac{12}{16}$

As a consequence of knowing the relation $\dfrac{a}{b} = \dfrac{n \times a}{n \times b}$, students can now visually and numerically compare two fractions with different denominators by creating common denominators relative to the same whole (**4.NF.2**). For example, their earlier visual experiences with unit fractions should easily convince them that $\dfrac{1}{2} > \dfrac{1}{3}$ relative to the same whole. In numerical terms, the relationship is also true because $\dfrac{1 \times 3}{2 \times 3} > \dfrac{1 \times 2}{3 \times 2}$, or $\dfrac{3}{6} > \dfrac{2}{6}$.

In practical terms, both requirements of comparing fractions relative to the same whole piece and converting to equivalent fractional forms that have the same denominator should enable fourth-grade students to progressively transition to a numerical process for comparing any pair of fractions. For example, a numerical processing of fraction tasks that have the same numerator (**4.NF.2**) such as $\frac{5}{2}$? $\frac{5}{3}$ involves initially creating common denominators. So,

$$\frac{5}{2}\times\frac{3}{3} \ ? \ \frac{5}{3}\times\frac{2}{2}$$

$$\frac{15}{6} \ ? \ \frac{10}{6}.$$

From the equivalent forms, $\frac{5}{2}>\frac{5}{3}$ since there are more sixth pieces on the left than on the right. Alternatively, $\frac{5}{2}>\frac{5}{3}$ since $2\frac{1}{2}>1\frac{2}{3}$.

Work with a pair and address the following four tasks below.

a. What units are used to compare the two fractions above in two different ways?

b. Lamar, 4th grader, makes the following claim: "*I'm thinking that in the case of 5/2 and 5/3, I really don't need to use the numerical process. I know that halves will always be bigger in size than thirds relative to the same whole, so 5 of halves should be greater than 5 of thirds.*" Does Lamar's reasoning make sense? Can you generalize his claim to all problems of the same type? Explain.

c. Standard 4.NF.2 also recommends having students compare fractions relative to a benchmark fraction such as $\frac{1}{2}$. Consider, for example, the task $\frac{5}{6}$? $\frac{2}{5}$. Since $\frac{5}{6}$ is greater than $\frac{1}{2}$ and $\frac{2}{5}$ is less than $\frac{1}{2}$, then $\frac{5}{6}>\frac{2}{5}$. Discuss advantages of and issues with this particular approach.

d. Marianne, Lamar's classmate, asked her father to help her try to make sense of comparing fractions. The next day, she shared with her classmates the following strategy: "*I know a super quick way to compare fractions. My father taught me to cross multiply. So,* $\frac{5}{6}>\frac{2}{5}$ *because 5 × 5, which equals 25, is greater than 2 × 6, which equals 12.*" Discuss advantages of and issues with this particular approach.

By the end of fourth grade, all students should know the following types of fractions $\frac{a}{b}$, where a is a whole number, $b \neq 0$, and b is restricted to whole numbers 2, 3, 4, 5, 6, 8, 10, 12, and 100:

- unit fractions if $a = 1$;
- proper fractions if $a < b$;
- whole numbers if $b = 1$;
- 1 if $a = b$;
- improper fractions if $a \geq b$.

e. What happens if $b = 0$? $a = b = 0$?

Fourth-grade students should also understand that fractions of the form $\dfrac{a}{b}$ are multiplicative expressions, as follows;

$$\frac{a}{b} \text{ means } a \text{ multiples of } \frac{1}{b}$$

$$\frac{a}{b} = \frac{1}{b} + \frac{1}{b} + \cdots + \frac{1}{b} = a \times \frac{1}{b}$$

$$\underbrace{\qquad\qquad\qquad}_{a \text{ times}}$$

Because of the multiplicative structure of fractions, students need to understand the central role that common units play in such a structure. Having a common unit, in fact, enables them to decompose fractions into sums of fractions in several different ways (**4.NF.3b**). The graphic organizer for $\dfrac{5}{6}$ shown in Figure 7.13 helps students see connections among the different representations for the same fraction. Do the following activity below.

f. Name a proper fraction and make a graphic organizer similar to the one shown in Figure 7.13.

In the case of an improper fraction that does not simplify to a whole number, having a firm understanding of *common unit* should help students see why its equivalent form results into a *mixed number* that involves the sum of a whole number and a proper fraction. For example, the improper fraction $\dfrac{11}{10}$ can be decomposed as $\dfrac{10}{10} + \dfrac{1}{10}$, which is equivalent to the mixed number form $1\dfrac{1}{10}$. The mixed expression $q\dfrac{a}{b}$ is a shortcut for $q + \dfrac{a}{b}$ and not $q \times \dfrac{a}{b}$, assuming that $\dfrac{1}{b}$ is the common unit. Work with a pair and do the following tasks below.

g. Martina and Drew, 4th graders, offered the following responses below when they were asked to describe the visual representation shown in Figure 7.14.

101

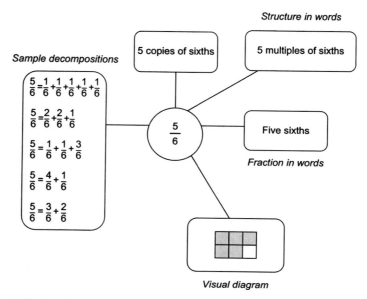

Figure 7.13. Graphic organizer showing different representations of a proper fraction

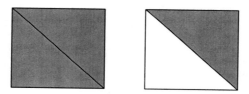

Figure 7.14. What do you see?

Martina: *It's* $\frac{3}{2}$.

Drew: *No, it's* $\frac{3}{4}$.

How would you address this issue in class?

Does Roman's explanation in relation to Figure 7.14 make sense? Why or why not? If it make sense, what can you learn from Roman's way of thinking that can inform the way you teach mathematics?

> *My common unit is a whole piece, and I see 2 whole pieces. But the second whole piece tells me it's a half. So I think it's* $1\frac{1}{2}$. *If I were to think like Martina, my common unit is a half, so 2 halves and a half gives*

me three halves, $\frac{3}{2}$. If I were to agree with Drew, my common unit would

be a fourth, so 1 fourth, 2 fourths, three fourths, $\frac{3}{4}$.

h. Use Roman's visual processing in wholes to help you convert $5\frac{1}{3}$ into an improper fraction. Then use Martina's visual processing in unit fractions as a second solution strategy. Which method makes sense, and why?

i. Jake, 4th grader, makes the following claim: "*To convert a mixed number into an improper fraction, my mother told me to simply multiply the denominator and the whole number, add the numerator, and copy the denominator. This "MAD" strategy always works.*" Discuss advantages of, and potential issues with, this strategy.

j. How does skip counting help students convert an improper fraction to its mixed form? Illustrate with an example.

Fourth grade students who understand decomposing fractions into sums and differences of fractions with the same denominator can easily deal with addition and subtraction of fractions that involve joining and separating parts relative to the same whole (**4.NF.3a, 4.NF.3c,** and **4.NF.3d**). Work with a pair and provide solutions to problems (*k*) through (*p*). Show both processing and translation aspects in every solution.

k. Marina divided a basket of fruits into sixths. Art kept $\frac{1}{6}$ of the basket. Bert kept $\frac{2}{6}$ of the basket. Corky kept $\frac{1}{6}$ of the basket. Marina kept the rest. What fractional part of the basket did Marina keep for herself?

l. Mr. Cruz divided a whole cake into sixths. Amelia ate $\frac{1}{6}$ of the cake. Bert ate $\frac{2}{6}$ of the cake. Mr. Cruz ate the rest of the cake. What fractional part of the cake did he eat?

m. Dwayne bought a bag of walnuts. Emily ate $\frac{1}{5}$ of the bag. Faye ate $\frac{2}{5}$ of the bag. How much of the bag did Emily and Faye eat?

n. One fourth of the cars in Parking Lot M are red. Two fourths of the cars are blue. The rest of the cars are black. What fraction of the cars is black?

o. The red squirrel ate $\frac{2}{10}$ of the acorns. The gray squirrel ate $\frac{3}{8}$ of the acorns. What fraction of the acorns did they eat altogether?

p. Miranda has two cats, Mimi and Didi. Everyday, Mimi eats $\dfrac{3}{8}$ of a can of food.

Didi eats twice that amount. How much of the can the two cats eat together?

q. Find different ways of adding and subtracting mixed numbers with the same denominators (**4.NF.3c**). Can you use them to add and subtract combinations of mixed numbers and proper fractions with the same denominators? Should all the different ways be taught in class? Discuss advantages and issues.

Since fractions are multiplicative expressions, the transition to the simple case of fraction multiplication is reasonable, that is, when the multiplier is a whole number (**4.NF.4**). Do the following activities below.

r. Find each product visually and numerically: (1) $4 \times \dfrac{2}{3}$; (2) $2 \times 1\dfrac{1}{2}$.

s. Refer to the content standard 4.NF.4c of the CCSSM on p. 30. Solve the multiplication problem.

Show both processing and translation aspects in your solution.

One interesting application of equivalent fractions involves relating fractions and decimals (**4.NF.5**). Fourth grade students learn decimal numbers as decimal fractions. When they learn to read and write decimal numbers as fractions (see section 4.3b; **4.NF.6**), they also learn that comparing two decimals to the hundredths place should refer to the same whole (**4.NF.7**). In the case of addition (and subtraction) of two decimal fractions, their ability to obtain equivalent fractions should help them deal with situations involving combinations of tenths and hundredths (see section 6.6; **4.NF.5**). They should also be able to visualize simple decimal fractions and locate them on a number line.

7.5 FRACTION ADDITION, SUBTRACTION, MULTIPLICATION, AND SIMPLE DIVISION IN GRADE 5

In fifth grade, students continue to use equivalent fractions to add and subtract proper and improper fractions with unlike denominators in both contextualized and decontextualized situations (**5.NF.1** and **5.NF.2**).

There are two interesting developments on fractions in fifth grade, as follows:

− The concept of fractions in the earlier grades emphasizes fractions as objects with a multiplicative structure. In fifth grade, the fraction concept is extended to convey an operation, that is, in terms of division of a numerator by a denominator, $\dfrac{a}{b} = a \div b$, where a and b are whole numbers and $b \neq 0$ (**5.NF.3**).

− Consequently, reconceptualizing fractions in terms of division enables students to explore problems that involve equal sharing.

For example, consider the following equal sharing problem below.

If 5 whole rectangular pizzas are shared equally among 6 people, how much is each person's share?

The problem translates into the following division expression: $5 \div 6$. Figure 7.15 shows a visual processing of the problem. Intuitively, you can partition each whole rectangular piece into 6 shares. In fact, many students in the lower elementary grades employ this strategy in the absence of formal instruction.

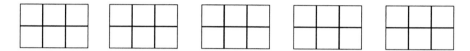

Figure 7.15. Partitioning each whole into six shares

Since each person is expected to receive a sixth share from each whole piece, then the person's total share is $5 \times \dfrac{1}{6} = \dfrac{5}{6}$. Hence, $5 \div 6 = 5 \times \dfrac{1}{6} = \dfrac{5}{6}$. You can verify that this answer is correct by multiplication, that is, $6 \times \dfrac{5}{6} = 5$ (why?). With a sufficient number of similar everyday examples, students should be able to verify that, indeed,

$$a \div b = a \times \frac{1}{b} = \frac{a}{b},$$

where a and b are whole numbers and $b \neq 0$. It is important to emphasize academic language at this stage. That is, dividing by 6 and multiplying by $\dfrac{1}{6}$ convey the same mathematical action. Work with a pair and do the following task below.

a. Access the link http://www.illustrativemathematics.org/standards/k8. Open the Number and Operations – Fractions page. Click on the Grade 5 link. Then open the "Show all" page and click the link "see illustrations" under B.3. Solve the task called *What is 23 ÷ 5?*

b. Knowing that $a \div b = a \times \dfrac{1}{b}$, it is reasonable to extend the values of a and b to include unit fractions. However, standard **5.NF.7** does not include division of a fraction by a fraction, which students pursue in sixth grade. Follow the procedure in (a) and access the following tasks below. Solve them completely and pay careful attention to both processing and translation aspects of your work.

1. Dividing a unit fraction by a nonzero whole number: Click the link "see illustrations" under 7.a and solve the problem *Painting a Room*.
2. Dividing a whole number by a unit fraction: Click the link "see illustrations" under 7.b and solve the problem *Origami Stars*.

Students in fourth grade use the definition of multiplication of two whole numbers to establish multiplication of a whole number (as a multiplier) and a fraction. In fifth grade, they deal with the remaining cases, that is, when the multiplier is a fraction and when both factors are fractions. Multiplication as repeated addition can still be made to work in cases when the multiplier is a fraction. For example, the expression $\frac{1}{6} \times 5$ as "5 repeated $\frac{1}{6}$ times" obviously does not make any sense. However, if we interpret it as "$\frac{1}{6}$ group of 5," that seems to be reasonable and can in fact be illustrated in a valid visual manner, as follows.

In third grade, students conceptualize multiplication of two whole numbers in terms of "equal groups or sets of." Since multiplication as scaling is introduced in fifth grade (**5.NF.5**), scaling can be extended to include scalar multipliers. Consequently, there should be no trouble interpreting the meaning of the operation $\times$ in terms of "equal groups of." Figure 7.16 shows a few examples, including "a part of a partition" interpretation as an alternative model for thinking about multiplication involving a fraction multiplier (**5.NF.4a**).

In the case of the product $\frac{a}{b} \times \frac{c}{d}$, the repeated-addition conception of whole number multiplication fails. However, you can still use either the equal group or the part of a partition model to help you develop a reasonable rule. Consider, for example, the task of obtaining the product of $\frac{1}{2} \times \frac{2}{3}$. In Figure 7.17, if you take 1 part of a partition of $\frac{2}{3}$ into 2 equal parts, then you obtain $\frac{1}{3}$. Alternatively, if you take a half of $\frac{2}{3}$, you also obtain $\frac{1}{3}$. Either way, $\frac{1}{2} \times \frac{2}{3} = \frac{1}{3}$.

You can also use an area model as an alternative approach to help students understand multiplication involving two fractions. Consider once again the task of obtaining the product of $\frac{1}{2} \times \frac{2}{3}$. Draw a unit square (i.e., a square with unit dimensions) and shade two parts when you partition it into three equal (horizontal) parts (see Figure 7.18). Next obtain $\frac{1}{2}$ of $\frac{2}{3}$, which means take 1 part when you partition $\frac{2}{3}$ into two equal (vertical) parts. So, $\frac{1}{2} \times \frac{2}{3} = \frac{2}{6}$ or $\frac{1}{3}$.

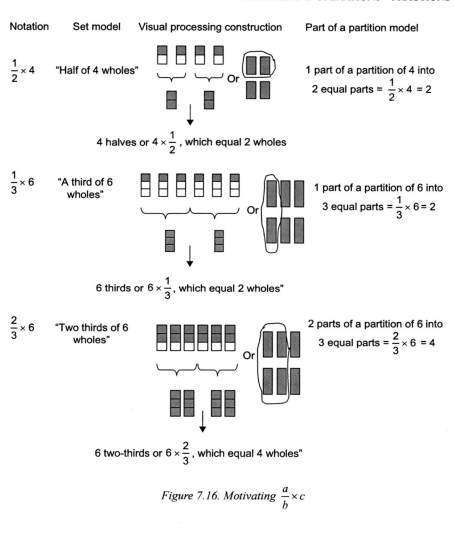

Figure 7.16. Motivating $\frac{a}{b} \times c$

Figure 7.17. 1 Part of a partition of $\frac{2}{3}$ *into 2 equal parts or an equal half of* $\frac{2}{3}$

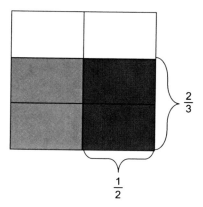

Figure 7.18. Area model for $\frac{1}{2} \times \frac{2}{3}$

A third approach involves *tiling* (**5.NF.4b**). Begin with a rectangular tile that has unit fractional dimensions $\frac{1}{3} \times \frac{1}{2}$ (refer to Figure 7.18). Use 6 such tiles to completely cover a unit square. Hence, a rectangle with height $\frac{2}{3}$ and width $\frac{1}{2}$ yields an area of $\frac{2}{6}$ or $\frac{1}{3}$, which illustrates $\frac{2}{3} \times \frac{1}{2} = \frac{2}{6} = \frac{1}{3}$.

The preceding three visual models should help fifth-grade students understand how $\frac{a}{b} \times \frac{c}{d} = \frac{ac}{bd}$. where b and $d \neq 0$. Work with a pair and do the following tasks below

c. Find the product of $\frac{5}{4} \times \frac{2}{5}$ in three different ways.

d. Create four story multiplication problems involving the equation $a \times b = c$ with the additional conditions noted under (i) through (iv). Then solve them using any method of your choice.

　　(i.)　both factors are whole numbers;
　　(ii.)　both factors are proper fractions;
　　(iii.)　a is a proper fraction and b is a mixed number; and
　　(iv.)　b is a proper fraction and a is a mixed number.

e. Authors Tom Parker and Scott Baldridge suggest that if we try to multiply two fractions in the same way that we add two fractions, that is,

$$\frac{a}{b} \times \frac{c}{b} = \frac{a \times c}{b}$$

then that test rule fails to satisfy at least one arithmetic property of multiplication. Consequently, it is not a valid rule. Which of the following properties of multiplication are not satisfied: commutativity; associativity; distributive property of multiplication over addition; and multiplicative identity?

f. Fifth grade students learn to associate multiplication with *scaling* or *resizing* (**5.NF.5**). Use numbers, rectangles, or on a number line to establish a conjecture about each situation below. Verify with a few examples.

    1. Start with any number. What we can conclude about the product when we multiply the number by a fraction greater than 1?

    2. Start with any number. What we can conclude about the product when we multiply the number by a fraction smaller than 1?

    3. Start with any number. What we can conclude about the product when we multiply the number by a fraction equal to $\frac{n}{n}$, where n is a counting number? *Counting numbers* are whole numbers excluding 0.

    4. Access the link http://www.illustrativemathematics.org/standards/k8. Open the Number and Operations – Fractions page. Click on the Grade 5 link. Then open the "Show all" page and click the link "see illustrations" under B.5. Solve all six tasks by drawing on the verified conjectures you established in item (e) above.

g. Search the internet for free online apps and games that deal with the topics in this section and assess potential benefits and possible concerns.

7.6 MAPPING THE CONTENT STANDARDS WITH THE PRACTICE STANDARDS

Work with a pair to accomplish the following task: Use the checklist you developed in Table 2.3 to map each content standard under the *NF* domain with the appropriate practice standards and NRC proficiency strands. Make a structure similar to the one shown in Table 3.2 to organize and record your responses.

7.7 DEVELOPING A CONTENT STANDARD PROGRESSION TABLE FOR THE NUMBER AND OPERATIONS – FRACTIONS DOMAIN

Continue working on your own domain table. Add the appropriate number of rows corresponding to your grade-level *NF* domain standards. Then map a reasonable content trajectory for each standard over the indicated timeline. Make sure that the different grade-level content standard progressions involving the *OAT*, *NBT*, and *NF* domains are coherently developed.

GEOMETRY

In this chapter, you will deal with content-practice, teaching, and learning issues relevant to elementary geometry in the *Geometry* (G) domain from kindergarten (K) through grade 5 of the CCSSM. Taken together, the the content standards illustrate how elementary students' conceptualization of geometric objects is expected to progress from recognizing and manipulating shapes in K to establishing and reasoning about figural properties in fifth grade. From a psychological perspective, their thinking can be viewed as evolving from perceiving objects in global terms in K to visualizing details about their defining attributes and integrating their geometrical and featural attributes by the time they complete fifth grade. For example, in K they name and describe 2D flat objects such as circles and rectangles and 3D solids such as cubes and cones in terms of their overall shapes. In fifth grade, they describe and classify various kinds of parallelograms in terms of their essential attributes that distinguish them from circles and other quadrilaterals. Also in fifth grade, students begin to explore the rectangular coordinate system, where points as locations in space are described in terms of ordered pairs of numbers. Table 8.1 lists the appropriate pages for your convenience.

Table 8.1. CCSSM Pages for the G Domain

Grade Level Domain	Standards	Page Numbers in the CCSSM
K.G	1 to 6	12
1.G	1 to 3	16
2.G	1 to 3	20
3.G	1 to 2	26
4.G	1 to 3	32
5.G	1 to 4	38

Make a wordle of terms that capture the *G* content standards. Access the link http://www.wordle.net/ to create your wordle. Remember that repetitions of the same word are allowed and need to be recorded as many times as they appear. When you are done constructing your own geometry wordle, share it with others. Which terms appear to be more prominent than others?

8.1 RECOGNIZING AND COMPOSING SHAPES IN KINDERGARTEN AND GRADE 1

K students' entry to formal geometry involves learning the names of different 2D and 3D shapes in various locations, positions, and orientations (**K.G.1** and **K.G.2**).

They also begin to describe their superficial features (**K.G.3** and **K.G.4**) that should help them when they compose larger shapes (**K.G.5** and **K.G.6**). Work with a pair and do the following activities below.

a. Identify all geometric objects and terms that K students need to learn before moving on to first grade.

b. Find online resources that will help K students learn about 2D and 3D shapes by singing about them. Assess the quality of the resources in terms of their potential in assisting K students learn the appropriate K *G* standards. Are the resources appropriate for English learners?

c. Access the following link below.

   http://www.mensaforkids.org/lessons/Shapes/MFKLessons-Shapes-All.pdf

   Refer to p. 1-1. Obtain a copy of one of the five books about shapes. Does the content satisfy the K standards under the *G* domain?

   Choose one of the remaining lessons (from 2 to 5) and modify it to align with the K *G* standards.

d. Access the following link below.

   http://catalog.mathlearningcenter.org/files/pdfs/PBLCCSSK2-0412w.pdf

   Modify the two activities for K students so that the new ones are aligned with the K *G* standards. What potential issues might they have in composing simple shapes to form larger shapes (**K.G.6**)?

e. Access the following link below.

   http://www.math-aids.com/Kindergarten/

   Which K worksheets can you use to teach the content standards? Which content standards apply? What makes them "great classroom activities" for K students?

f. Access the following article below.

   Clements, D., Wilson, D., & Sarama, J. (2004). Young children's composition of geometric figures: A learning trajectory. *Mathematical thinking and learning, 6*(2), 163–184.

   Focus on Table 1 (p. 168), which shows young children's progression of competence for the composition of shapes beginning at age 4. Which levels in the progression are K students able to achieve?

In first grade, students continue to use 2D and 3D shapes to form new composite shapes and create more shapes from fully formed composite shapes (**1.G.2**). Their level of attention and description also transitions from associating shapes with whole objects to differentiating between defining and nondefining attributes, enabling them to create new shapes on the basis of the defining attributes (**1.G.1**). Continue to work with your pair and do the following task below.

g. Refer to the reference in item (e). Which level in the progression are students expected to achieve by the end of first grade?

Read the entire article. Discuss at least three results from the authors' study that you think are interesting to know relative to kindergarten and first grade students' proficiency in composing shapes. What problems might they have in learning to compose and decompose shapes? Give examples to illustrate such problems. What do the authors say about the significance of young children's competence with shapes in relation to the other CCSSM domains?

h. Access the following article below.

Brown, C. (2009). More than just number. *Teaching Children Mathematics*, *15*(8), 474–479.

How does the author characterize good environments that support quality instruction and growth in young children's geometric knowledge? Name and describe a few examples of such environments.

i. Access the following article below.

Cross, D., Adefope, O., Lee, M. Y., & Perez, A. (2012). Hungry for Early Spatial and Algebraic Reasoning. *Teaching Children Mathematics, 19*(1), 42–49.

The authors describe participating teachers' accounts of K and first-grade students who engaged in spatial-reasoning activities with pattern blocks using two story contexts that motivated them to compose and decompose shapes. Describe how the classroom sessions were orchestrated and the teacher actions that supported the development of children's spatial-reasoning skills.

Focus on the algebraic activity that provided first-grade students with an opportunity to generate and describe shape and numerical patterns involving a growing caterpillar. The authors carefully described the emergence of students' recursive rules and their relative inability to express those rules as direct expressions. According to the authors, "(i)dentifying and describing direct expressions are often difficult for first graders because most students are not multiplicative reasoners at this age" (p. 48). Check the content standards mappings that you developed in the previous chapters to assess whether this argument makes sense. At what stage in the CCSSM are students expected to show proficiency in constructing tables and direct expressions for shape and numerical patterns?

h. In section 7.1, you explored standards **1.G.3, 2.G.2, 2.G.3** and **3.G.2** in relation to beginning fraction learning. How is partitioning action connected to decomposing geometric figures? Is decomposition limited to equal partitioning? Why or why not?

113

8.2 DEFINING AND REASONING ABOUT SHAPES IN GRADES 2, 3, AND 5

Standards **2.G.1, 3.G.1, 4.G, 5.G.3,** and **5.G.4** deal with figural property discernment and construction that further support deep structure or concept attainment. This means that representations of geometric objects are provided with analytic descriptions in terms of their defining attributes. Work with pair and do the following tasks below.

  a. Check the CCSSM and carefully identify all geometric objects that second-grade students need to learn. What recommended attributes are appropriate at their level?
  b. In third and fifth grade, students explore different kinds of quadrilaterals. Search online resources that show relationships between and among the different kinds of quadrilaterals.
  c. Establishing *definitions* is an important structuring activity in the elementary school mathematics curriculum. Access the following link below to learn about the difference between stipulated versus extracted definitions. Answer the questions that follow.

  http://ir.library.oregonstate.edu/xmlui/bitstream/handle/1957/21549/EdwardsB arbara.Mathematics.Role%20of%20MathematicalDefinitions.pdf?sequence=1

     (i) Focus on pp. 224–225: What kind of definition is acceptable in mathematics, and why? Focus on p. 229: What are the pedagogical objectives of activities that focus on establishing and understanding definitions? Explain how classifying quadrilaterals involves knowing both necessary and preferred features.
     (ii) The 2D geometric objects that students pursue in second and third grade exemplify polygons. Establish a stipulated definition for the term *polygon.*
       Examples and *nonexamples* are also used to help students establish and understand definitions. Examples exhibit all the stipulated attributes in a definition, while nonexamples include some but not all of them. Determine examples and nonexamples of polygons. Also, establish a stipulated definition for a *cube* and generate examples and nonexamples.
     (iii) Develop appropriate definition activities for second-, third-, and fifth-grade students that will help them understand the following classifications: (a) kinds of triangles by their side lengths; (b) kinds of triangles by their angles; and (c) kinds of quadrilaterals. Pay careful attention to the stipulated content standards at each grade level.

8.3 LINES AND ANGLES IN 2D SHAPES IN GRADE 4

In fourth grade, students learn about lines, subsets of lines, parallel and perpendicular lines, angles, and different kinds of angles **(4.G.1)**. Knowing these basic geometric objects and their characteristics should enable them to define and classify 2D figures by their sides and angles in precise terms (**4.G.2**). They also formally define, construct, and investigate lines of symmetry in 2D figures (**4.G.3**).

Work with a pair and do the following tasks below.

a. Search online resources that will help fourth grade students learn about points and lines and their subsets. Check to see if the following terms are included in the discussion: points and their labels; lines and their labels; segments and their labels; half lines and their labels; and rays and their labels. What problems might they encounter?

b. Search online for a definition of an angle. How is it usually labeled? Does it include the interior arc that refers to its measure? Explain.

c. Fourth-grade teacher Mr. Lester defined an angle in the following manner below.

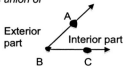

Here is angle ABC (Figure 8.1). It consists of the union of two rays BA and BC that share a common endpoint, B. Notice that ∠ABC separates the plane or flat surface into three parts, the interior part, the exterior part, and the the angle itself, which consists of the points on ∠ABC.

Figure 8.1. Angle ABC

Mr. Lester then asked his students to show him examples of angles on their mini whiteboard. Two students, Michaela and Kevin, eagerly raised their hands and shared with the class their drawn angles.

B   A = C

Figure 8.2. Michaela's angle ABC

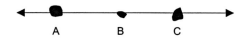

A   B   C

Figure 8.3. Kevin's angle ABC

Are the two angles acceptable by Mr. Lester's definition? Explain. Check to see if they satisfy the definition of an angle provided in standard **4.MD.5**.

d. Are angles and angle measures (e.g., right angles and acute angles) the same concept? Explain.

115

e. Standard **4.G.1** involves drawing right, acute, and obtuse angles. Are there other measures of angles that students should know? Explain.

f. If students do not have access to a set square, how can they use paperfolding to help them construct a right angle?

g. If fourth grade students know the concept of a right angle, how can they use it to define and construct parallel and perpendicular lines? Demonstrate with or without the aid of a set square.

h. If fourth grade students know the concepts of a right angle and parallel and perpendicular lines, they can use them to define and classify all quadrilaterals. Explain how they can accomplish the two tasks with the aid of geostrips.

i. If fourth grade students know the different kinds of angles, they can classify triangles according to their angle. How can they conceptualize them with the aid of geostrips?

j. Students informally learn about lines of symmetry in first grade (**1.G.3**). In fourth grade, how are they expected to formally define a line of symmetry?

k. Search interesting online activities that will help students use the concepts in this section in mathematical and everyday contexts.

8.4 THE COORDINATE PLANE IN GRADE 5

Students in fifth grade are introduced to the coordinate plane for the first time. Work with a pair and do the following tasks below.

a. The introduction to coordinate geometry in fifth grade is a conceptual shift from students' earlier experiences with geometric objects. What might have been the motivation for this new representation of geometry? Conduct an online search that will help you understand differences between analytic and Euclidean geometry. Describe elementary students' initial geometric experiences in the lower grades. What purpose does analytic geometry serve in the upper grades?

b. What should fifth grade students know about the coordinate plane (**5.G.1**)? What issues might they have in relation to graphing points in the first quadrant of the coordinate plane (**5.G.2**)?

c. Search appropriate online activities that will help fifth-grade students become proficient in plotting points in a coordinate plane.

d. Access the link http://www.illustrativemathematics.org/standards/k8. Open the Geometry page. Click on the Grade 5 link. Then open the "Show all" page and click the link "see illustrations" under A.1. Solve the task called *Battle Ship Using Grid Paper*. What will students learn from solving the task?

e. Access the link below.

http://insidemathematics.org/common-core-math-tasks/5th-grade/
5-2007%20Granny's%20Balloon%20Trip.pdf.

Solve the *Granny's Balloon Trip* task. Identify possible issues that fifth grade students might have in relation to the task. How can you help them resolve those issues?

8.5 MAPPING THE CONTENT STANDARDS WITH THE PRACTICE STANDARDS

Work with a pair to accomplish the following task: Use the checklist you developed in Table 2.3 to map each content standard under the *G* domain with the appropriate practice standards and NRC proficiency strands. Make a structure similar to the one shown in Table 3.2 to organize and record your responses.

8.6 DEVELOPING A CONTENT STANDARD PROGRESSION TABLE FOR GEOMETRY DOMAIN

Continue working on your own domain table. Add the appropriate number of rows corresponding to your grade-level *G* domain standards. Then map a reasonable content trajectory for each standard over the indicated timeline. Make sure that the different grade-level content standard progressions involving the *OAT*, *NBT*, *NF*, and *G* domains are coherently developed.

CHAPTER 9

MEASUREMENT AND DATA

In this chapter, you will deal with content-practice, teaching, and learning issues relevant to the *Measurement and Data* (MD) domain from kindergarten (K) through grade 5 of the CCSSM. The measurement clusters build on multiplicative structures, while the data clusters focus on ways in which data can be organized and reasonably interpreted around well-defined structures. Table 9.1 lists the appropriate pages for your convenience.

Table 9.1. CCSSM Pages for the MD Domain

Grade Level Domain	Standards	Page Numbers in the CCSSM
K.MD	1 to 3	12
1.MD	1 to 4	16
2.MD	1 to 10	20
3.MD	1 to 8	24–25
4.MD	1 to 7	31–32
5.MD	1 to 5	37

Take a moment to learn a few things about the *MD* domain by making a wordle of terms. Access the link http://www.wordle.net/ to create a wordle. In the box where it tells you to "paste in a bunch of text," remember that repetitions of the same word are allowed and should, thus, be recorded as many times as they appear. When you are done constructing your own MD wordle, share it with others. Which terms appear to be more prominent than others?

9.1 MEASURING FROM KINDERGARTEN TO GRADE 5

Work with a pair and provide a response to the following two related questions below.

a. What does it mean to measure in mathematics? What does it mean to engage in measurement thinking in school mathematics?

9.1.1 Qualitative Measurements in Kindergarten

K students begin their formal measurement experiences by determining the lengths, weights, and other measurable attributes of objects using nonstandard measures (e.g.: pencils, erasers, hands, feet, cubes, etc.; **K.MD. 1**). They also learn to compare and describe differences between two objects in terms of a common measurable attribute. In comparing, they begin to use terms such as *shorter* and *taller, more of* and *less of, longer* and *shorter*, *light* and *heavy*, etc. (**K.MD.2**). All explorations take place in the context of hands-on experiences involving everyday, real, and other concrete objects. Continue working with your pair and do the following tasks below.

  a. Search online resources that describe measurement activities for K students. Identify teaching tips that you can draw from the activities. Share ideas and activities that surprise you.
  b. What insights do K students obtain from measuring objects using nonstandard measurements? Also, what potential issues can occur? Suggest ways that can resolve the issues.

9.1.2 Measuring Lengths in Grades 1 and 2

In first grade, students continue to compare objects by length and compare the lengths of two objects indirectly by employing a third object (**1.MD.1**). Further, the task of measuring the length of a single object, say, O, can be used to introduce students to multiplicative thinking. For instance, have students use a smaller object, say, s, as a unit length to measure the total length of O (**1.MD.2**). The repeated use of s – that is, laying down copies of s from end to end with no gaps or overlaps - exemplifies the visual processing that characterizes the basic structure of measuring in any context. The converted expression is a number, which in third grade can be expressed as a multiplicative expression. Indeed, and more generally speaking, measuring a known attribute of an object involves visually iterating an explicit unit from side to side with no gaps or overlaps and translating the process in numerical form. Do the following task below.

  a. Access the article, *Measurement of Length: The Need for a Better Approach to Teaching*, from the following site below.

  https://sites.google.com/site/constancekamii/articles-available-for-printing

  How is the article related to standard 1.MD.1? What is the significance of transitive reasoning and unit iterating in the early development of students' thinking regarding measurement of lengths? What recommendations do the authors suggest in terms of how kindergarten and first-grade children can be taught to compare lengths of objects that make sense to them?

In second grade, students determine the length of an object standard measurement tools (e.g., rulers, yardsticks, meter sticks, measuring tapes; **2.MD.1**) and standard units (e.g., inches, feet, centimeters, and meters; **2.MD.3**). They also compare measurements of the same length using different standard measures (**2.MD.2**) and the lengths of two objects in terms of the same standard measure (**2.MD.4**). Further, they solve addition and subtraction word problems up to 100 involving lengths that use the same unit length measure (**2.MD.5**). By the end of second grade, they should be able to construct a number line diagram of whole numbers – that is, a ruler with equally spaced points that correspond to 0, 1, 2, 3, … – and perform addition and subtraction up to 100 (**2.MD.6**).

Work with a pair and do the following task below.

a. What is the difference between a ruler and a straightedge?
b. Access the link http://www.illustrativemathematics.org/standards/k8. Open the MD page. Click on the Grade 1 link. Then open the "Show all" page and click the link "see illustrations" under A.2. Check all three tasks and read the anticipated student actions and commentaries. Identify potential issues that first grade students might have within and across the three tasks.
c. Follow the steps in (a) above and analyze the tasks shown under 2.MD.A and 2.MD.B.
d. Which standards in the third grade CCSSM require standard 2.MD.6?
e. Search the internet for free online apps and games that pertain to the topics in this section and assess potential benefits and possible concerns.

9.1.3 Finding Perimeters and Measuring Lengths with Halves and Fourths of an Inch, Areas, and Estimating Liquid Volumes and Masses of Objects in Standard Units in Grade 3

In third grade, students continue to measure lengths of objects with the aid of a ruler that has markings of halves and fourths of an inch (**3.MD.4**). Then they use their developing expertise with rulers and arithmetical skills in adding and subtracting whole numbers to either calculate the perimeter of a particular polygon or find an unknown side length of the polygon (**3.MD.8**). Remember that the perimeter of a polygon refers to the total length of the side lengths of the polygon. Work with a pair and do the following tasks below.

a. What possible issues might third-grade students have in working through each task shown in Figure 9.1? What can you do to help them overcome those issues?
b. Modify the numbers on each task shown in Figure 9.1 so that they are appropriate for fourth grade students (**4.MD.3**).

Also in third grade, students begin to explore nonlinear measurement tasks such as finding the exact areas of certain plane figures (**3.MD.5** to **3.MD.7**) and estimating the volumes and masses of objects using standard units of grams, kilograms, and liters (**3.MD.2**). They also solve word problems involving linear and nonlinear measurements. Their measurement thinking at this stage should enable them to distinguish between linear and area measures, which can be assessed through activities that ask them to construct rectangles that have either the same perimeter

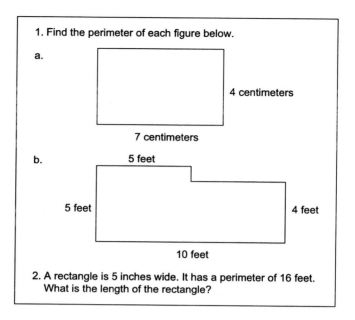

Figure 9.1. Perimeter tasks for third grade students

and different areas or the same area and different perimeters (**3.MD.8**). Continue working with your pair and do the following tasks below.

c. Determine the perimeter and area of the figure shown in Figure 9.2 What issues might third-grade students have in solving the problem, and what can you do to help them?

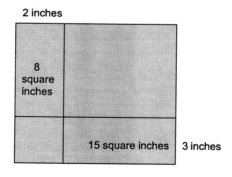

Figure 9.2. Combined perimeter-area task for third grade students

d. Construct two rectangles that have the same perimeter but different areas.

e. Construct two rectangles that have the same area but different perimeters.

One interesting way to teach area in third grade involves *tiling* or *tesellating* a plane figure with tiles in such a way that no two tiles share any interior points and that the tiles together are able to completely cover the figure. When you demonstrate tiling with students, you need to emphasize that there ought to be no gaps between any pair of tiles. That is, tiling has to be constructed in a side-to-side manner, where each side of one tile is a side of one neighboring tile. Give them a rectangular sheet of paper and ask them to use pattern blocks to tile the sheet with: (1) equilateral triangles; (2) squares; (3) regular hexagons; (4) trapezoids; and (5) circles. Have them count the number of tiles that are needed to completely cover the sheet of paper in each case. It is important for them to experience at this stage the intuitive and visual meaning of *area*, which at least for now is restricted to *unit squares* (**3.MD.5**). As a consequence of their hands-on experiences, they should be able to distinguish between a unit square as a geometric object and 1 square unit as its area (**3.MD.5**). Further, with the aid of a ruler, have them construct different kinds of unit squares whose dimensions are expressed in centimeters, meter, inch, and foot (**3.MD.6**). They need to visually experience the difference between, say, a square centimeter and a square inch, a square inch and a square foot, etc. Work with a pair and do the following tasks below.

e. Carefully read standard **3.MD.7 a through c**. What is the recommended approach to finding the area of a rectangle with whole-number side lengths? How are standards 3.MD.7a, 3.MD.7b, and 3.MD.7c related to the concept and operation of multiplication in third grade?

f. Find the areas of the rectilinear figures shown in Figure 9.3 based on the recommended approach stated in **3.MD.7d**.

g. Search activities that will help third grade students estimate the volumes and masses of objects using standard units of grams, kilograms, and liters (**3.MD.2**). What does volume and mass mean? Go to section 9.1.5 for a more formal development of the concept of volumes involving cubes and other right rectangular prisms. Why is such an approach pursued in fifth grade (**5.MD.3 through 5.MD.5**) and not in third grade?

9.1.4 Measuring Angles in Grade 4

Consistent with the conceptual development of lengths and areas in the lower grades, measuring angles can also be explained in a multiplicative context. That is, a standard unit called *degree* is first constructed (**4.MD.5a**). Then multiple iterations or copies of 1-degree angles together comprise an angle measure of n degrees (**4.MD.5b**). Fourth-grade students also learn to measure angles and draw angles with particular measures with the aid of a protractor (**4.MD.6**). Work with a pair and do the following tasks:

a. Carefully read standard 4.MD.5a. What is the recommended way of developing the concept of a 1-degree angle? Are angle measures considered numbers? Explain. Define half turns, full turns, quarter turns, and three quarter turns in terms of degrees.

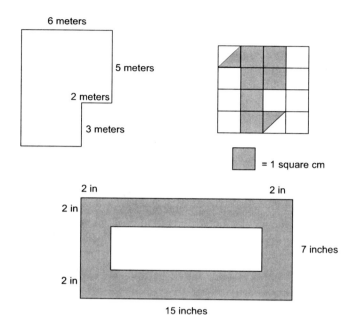

Figure 9.3. Rectilinear figures tasks for third grade students

b. Fourth grade students also engage in problem solving activities that involve angle measures (4.MD.7). Access the link below and open the MD page. Click on the Grade 4 link. Open the "Show all" page and "see illustrations" under C.7 and solve the Finding an unknown angle task.

http://www.illustrativemathematics.org/standards/k8

9.1.5 Measuring Volumes of Cubes and Other Right Rectangular Prisms in Grade 5

Work with a pair and do the following tasks below.

a. Carefully read standards **5.MD.3 through 5.MD.5.** How is exact volume measured in relation to students' experiences with cubes and other right rectangular prisms? Compare this cluster of standards with the cluster of standards for measuring exact areas in fourth grade. What are some conceptual implications of standard **5.MD.5b** in terms of how fifth grade students should learn solids, especially cubes and other right rectangular prisms?

Access the link below and solve the *How Many Cubes* task.
http://insidemathematics.org/common-core-math-tasks/5th-grade/5-2004%20
How%20Many%20Cubes.pdf

b. Access the link http://www.illustrativemathematics.org/standards/k8. Open the MD page. Click on the Grade 5 link. Then open the "Show all" page and click the link "see illustrations" under C. Solve the *Box of Clay* task. Solve as well the task shown in section C.5.b called *Carl's Aquarium*. What concepts, processes, and other relevant knowledge and skills do fifth-grade students need to have in order to successfully deal with such problems?

c. Search the internet for free online apps and games that deal with the topics in this section and assess potential benefits and possible concerns.

9.1.6 Conversion Problems in Grades 4 and 5

Work with a pair and do the tasks below.

a. Read standards **4.MD.1, 4.MD.2,** and **5.MD.1.** What prerequisite skills do fourth- and fifth-grade students need to have in order to be successful on tasks that assess them on these standards? What issues might they have with metric conversion?

b. Search appropriate online activities (e.g., games) that will help you teach measurement conversion in an interesting way.

9.2 TELLING AND WRITING TIME IN GRADES 2 AND 3

Work with a pair and do the following tasks below.

a. Trace the development of telling and writing time from second to third grade. Why is this particular topic classified under measurement? Does the concept of measuring time involve a multiplicative structure? Explain.

b. Access the following link below.

http://www.nsa.gov/academia/_files/collected_learning/elementary/geometry/elapsed_time.pdf

Solve all the problems under Student Resources and list potential issues that students might have.

c. Make sure you accomplish task (b) before you do this next task. Access the following article below by Constance Kamii and Kelly Russell.

Kamii, C. & Russell, K. (2012). Elapsed time: Why is it so difficult to teach? *Journal for Research in Mathematics Education, 43(3), 296–315.*

What difficulties do students usually have with elapsed time? What do you learn from the educational implications suggested in the article? What classroom activities will support growth in students' ability to deal with elapsed time tasks?

d. Search the internet for free online apps and games that pertain to the topics in this section and assess potential benefits and possible concerns.

9.3 MONEY IN GRADES 2 AND 4

Work with a pair and discuss the following question below.

a. Why is money classified under measurement?

When second grade students begin to explore tasks that ask them to recognize coins and their denominations, they need to develop a global sense of the shape and color of each coin in both physical and paper formats. Rushing them to remember the faces associated with the coins is not helpful at all. Also, asking them to identify paper versions of coins that do not resemble the actual size of the coins (e.g., a dime that is much bigger than a quarter) does not make sense. Providing them with laminated money cards is one effective way of assisting them to write both verbal and numerical representations of coins and their denominations correctly. Refer to Figure 3.3 for a sample of such cards involving whole numbers. In the case of money cards, you can make a front-and-back page that has the usual coins appearing on one side and the corresponding amount or value in both word and numerical formats with the appropriate symbols appearing on the other side of the page (**2.MD.8**). Once you have made the money cards, assemble them and use a screw lock ring to bind them together.

Obtaining total and equivalent amounts can be a difficult activity for many second-grade students since they are still in the process of coordinating their academic language and arithmetical strategies that will help them count efficiently and systematically. Work with a pair and do the following tasks below.

b. Check the relevant content standards in the other domains that you think second grade students need to know really well in order to accomplish the task of obtaining total and equivalent amounts.

c. How might you help second-grade students learn to obtain correct totals and equivalent amounts from sets of coins? Develop a plan and share with other pairs. Search online teaching tips as well.

Making change in second grade requires expertise in academic language, counting, and arithmetical strategies. In fourth grade, making change tasks involve using two or more arithmetical operations with larger values that consist of combinations of bills and coins and/or the use of two or more arithmetical operations (**4.MD.2**). Work with a pair and do the following tasks below.

d. What arithmetical strategies in second grade are appropriate to solve the following problem below?

> *Maria bought an eraser for 35¢. She gave 50¢ to pay for the eraser. How much change did Maria get? What coins did Maria get back?*

Modify the task so that it is appropriate for fourth-grade students.

9.4 CLASSIFYING, REPRESENTING, AND INTERPRETING DATA
FROM KINDERGARTEN TO GRADE 5

9.4.1 Forming Categories Involving Discrete Objects in Kindergarten

Work with a pair and do the following tasks below.

a. Read content standards K.MD.3 and 1.MD.4. How are K and first-grade students expected to understand the nature of discrete data?

9.4.2 Structuring Data from Kindergarten to Grade 5

Work with a pair and do the following tasks below.

a. Access at least three online resources and lessons on line plots. What mathematical content knowledge is required to obtain a full understanding of line plots? What potential issues might students have in constructing them?

b. Carefully study the MD content standards that pertain to the concept of line plots. Trace the development of students' understanding of line plots from second to fifth grade. Consider as well the types of problem tasks that are appropriate at each grade level.

c. Access the link http://www.scoe.org/files/mars-grade4.pdf and solve the *Texting* task on p. 106. Check the MD standards to determine grade level applicability.

d. Students also need to learn other kinds of graphs such as bar graphs, picture graphs, and box graphs. Investigate these concepts by following the same instructions in (a).

e. Access the link http://www.scoe.org/files/mars-grade4.pdf and solve the *Dinosaur Data* on p. 61 and the *Dinosaurs and Dragon* on p. 76. Check the MD standards to determine grade level applicability.

9.5 MAPPING THE CONTENT STANDARDS WITH THE PRACTICE STANDARDS

Work with a pair to accomplish the following task: Use the checklist you developed in Table 2.3 to map each content standard under the *MD* domain with the appropriate practice standards and NRC proficiency strands. Make a structure similar to the one shown in Table 3.2 to organize and record your responses.

9.6 DEVELOPING A CONTENT STANDARD PROGRESSION TABLE
FOR THE MEASUREMENT AND DATA DOMAIN

Continue working on your own domain table. Add the appropriate number of rows corresponding to your grade-level *MD* domain standards. Then map a reasonable content trajectory for each standard over the indicated timeline. Make sure that the different content standard progressions involving the *OAT, NBT, NF, G,* and *MD* domains are conceptually aligned and coherently developed.

CHAPTER 10

CONTENT-PRACTICE ASSESSMENT

In this chapter, you will learn different content-practice assessment strategies that will help you measure elementary students' understanding of the CCSSM. The term *measure* should not be conceptualized merely in terms of scaled values or proficiency labels relevant to performances on a content-practice standard being assessed. Think of *measure* in terms of patterns that students exhibit relative to the content-practice. Following Robert Mislevy, such patterns may indicate regularities that can tell you how they learn mathematics and provide you with information about various opportunities to learn and resources that are available to them before, during, and after assessment. In fact, when you engage with colleagues to study student work for a larger number of students, your findings will most likely yield interesting and relevant patterns that are useful in supporting improved and high-quality content-practice teaching and learning. Consequently, viewing assessment findings in terms of patterns will most likely vary from year to year, from classroom to classroom, and from student to student depending on circumstances that influence and shape performance on tasks.

In this chapter you will also learn to assess elementary students' content-practice proficiency in ways that are consistent with the structure of the Smarter Balanced Assessment (SBA). The SBAs have been referred to as the "next-generation assessments." They are meant to measure 21st century skills. They are also carefully aligned with the CCSSM. Further, they are intended to measure student progress towards college and career readiness, that is, the requisite mathematical competence that all students need to possess in order to succeed in entry-level credit-bearing coursework and a demanding high-skilled workforce. Each grade-level SBA, which begins in third grade and culminates in eleventh grade, consists of selected-response questions (e.g., multiple choice and true or false), constructed response items (e.g., draw a diagram and provide solutions), technology-enriched (i.e., computer-mediated) response items, and performance tasks. Performance tasks, especially, are meant to engage elementary students in in-depth projects that enable them to apply their analytical and real-world problem solving skills. Towards the end of the chapter, you will deal with alternative forms of assessment.

A good way to start thinking about content-practice assessment involves reflecting on your own experiences as students in math classrooms. Work with a group and address the following tasks below.

a. Reflect on your previous (student) experiences of testing in your favorite subject. What kinds of tests did you enjoy the most, and why? Which ones were difficult and/or challenging, and why? Think about the style and quality of math items that you had to answer. Was content prioritized over practice, or vice-versa? Or, was there a balance between content and practice? Remember "practice" is used here in the CCSSM context.

b. This time consider your experiences of testing in any of your previous math classes. Respond to the same questions listed in (a).

c. It is common knowledge that teachers tend to teach the way they were taught. Do you agree or disagree that the same thing can be claimed about testing, that is, "teachers tend to test the way they were tested?" Is that a good thing or an irresponsible practice?

d. Draw on the responses of your group to assemble possible dos and donts about testing. Then access the reference below to read Dylan William's view on assessment.

William, Dylan. (2006). Assessment. *Journal of Staff Development, 27*(1), 16–20.

Compare your responses with the author's general assessment-for-learning strategies. Which strategies on your list align with his suggested strategies? What new ideas are you eager to test?

When you assess students' mathematical proficiency in the CCSSM, you will need to use tasks that are framed around the content standards (i.e., Claim 1-assessment target items) and the eight practice standards (i.e., Claim 2-, 3-, and 4-assessment target items). For example, Figure 10.1 exemplifies a fifth-grade content-practice item under the *Number and Operations - Fractions* domain (i.e., 5.NF.7) that assesses at least one content standard and one practice standard. Both the style of testing and the thinking that is needed to accomplish the task depart from older and simpler content-driven assessments such as the one shown in Figure 10.2. Continue to work with your group and deal with the following task below.

e. Solve the two tasks shown in Figures 10.1 and 10.2. What content and practice standards are being assessed on each task? Carefully read content standard 5.NF.7 and William's five assessment-for-learning strategies. How might you use the assessment task in Figure 10.1 to develop learning intentions and success criteria with all students and orchestrate effective classroom discussions and tasks around similar items?

Fred's popcorn stand sells bags that weigh $\frac{2}{3}$ of a pound. Mrs. Telly wants to buy popcorn for her small class of fifth-grade students. She thinks she needs 8 pounds. How many students does she have? Choose the correct number.

A. $\frac{16}{3}$ B. $\frac{3}{16}$ C. 12   D. 16 $\frac{26}{3}$

Figure 10.1. Common-core practice standard question involving 5.NF.7

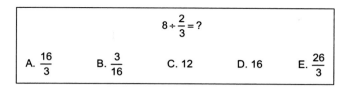

Figure 10.2. Traditional content-driven question involving 5.NF.7

10.1 GENERAL CONCEPTIONS SURROUNDING ASSESSMENT

Do the following tasks below that will help you construct an appropriate meaning of assessment in an educational context.

a. Search online for various meanings of assessment in an educational context. Access the link http://www.wordle.net/ to create a wordle. Paste in the wordle box at least **ten** different characterizations of assessment. When you are done constructing your own *assessment* wordle, generate initial impressions. For example, which terms in your wordle appear to be more prominent than others? Which terms caught your attention?

b. Share your wordle with a group of three other students. Work together to develop a definition of assessment. When you have formulated your group definition, consider once again your earlier individual responses to items (a) and (b) in the introduction. Assess the extent to which your personal experiences of assessment reflect various aspects of your group definition of assessment.

c. If your group is part of a whole class, assemble a gallery walk of group definitions of assessment. Then formulate a shared definition of assessment.

The preceding activity should give you a beginning grasp of the basic characteristics of assessment in an educational context. The following three valuable views regarding assessments, which have been drawn from the Gordon Commission report on the future of education, are also worth keeping in mind:

1. The troika of assessment, teaching, and learning forms the backbone of a well-conceptualized pedagogy. While the three processes can take place independently, their mutual coordination is necessary in order to guarantee meaningful pedagogical experiences for all students. The key is alignment. It is impossible in school contexts to conceptualize teaching that is not informed by any form of assessment of student learning. Further, both assessment and teaching should aim improved learning.

2. Assessment is a process of reasoning from evidence. However, it is also important to remember that evidence is imprecise to a certain extent. All findings from any kind of assessment basically provide an estimate of what students either know or are able to accomplish.

3. Fundamental to any assessment planning is a clearly articulated model of cognition and learning. You need to know the best evidence possible regarding how your students learn, process, and represent a target content standard and the relevant practice standards, including effective means that can support them attain proficiency in both content and practice standards.

To gain a mindset of alignment, work on the following task below with a group.

d. First, draw on your CCSSM domain tables and decide on a cluster of content standards that your group is interested in exploring together. Before you fill out Table 10.1, discuss the following concerns below.

   i. Identify a cluster (also called *Claim 1 assessment target* in SBA terms) that you are interested in assessing together. Specify a particular content standard in that cluster that is reasonable to assess in a single 50-minute classroom session.

   ii. Identify a practice standard that you also want to assess. Refer to your Table 2.3, which provides you with a checklist of specific actions (also called *Claim 2, 3, or 4 assessment targets* in SBA terms) under each practice standard. Specify one specific action that you intend to assess in relation to the content standard you identified in (i).

   iii. Describe an evidence that you need to establish that will indicate students' success in achieving the two assessment targets you intend to measure. What type of assessment items or tasks and task models are appropriate and will provide you with that evidence?

   iv. How might students go about learning the relevant content and practice standards that will enable them to exhibit mathematical proficiency in your planned assessment?

   v. How might teaching be orchestrated to support students' meaningful and successful learning of the articulated content and practice standards?

Regarding item (iii), an evidence statement that restates your content standard as a student-driven objective is sufficient. For example, an evidence statement for the task shown in Figure 10.1, which is based on the relevant content standard 5.NF.7b, can be as follows:

"*The student can interpret division of a whole number by a unit fraction and compute its quotient.*"

Assessment items can be drawn from any of the following sources below.

• Tasks that are aligned with district/benchmark and other released sample assessment items;
• Tasks that are aligned with current district and state standards and benchmarks.

Task models provide information about important features of assessment items or tasks that enable students to exhibit the stipulated evidence. Figure 10.1 is an example of a task model in which case students are presented with a division problem involving a whole-number dividend and a fraction divisor.

Regarding assessment items or tasks, develop or use those that model SBA tasks such as the ones noted below. Access the following link below, which will take you to the released SBA sample tasks, to help you gain a better understanding of each task description.

http://www.smarterbalanced.org/sample-items-and-performance-tasks/

– *Selected-response tasks* involve selecting one or more responses from a set of options (e.g., single- or multiple-response multiple choice items or true-or-false items);
– *Technology-enhanced tasks* target deeper understanding of content and skills that cannot be accomplished in the context of traditional tasks. For example, simulations that demonstrate mathematical phenomena provide students with an opportunity to engage in simple conceptual investigations and establish inferences within given constraints;
– *Constructed-response tasks* involve the construction of a detailed solution;
– *Performance tasks* integrate knowledge and skills across multiple content standards. They measure depth of understanding, research skills, and other forms of complex analysis that cannot be adequately assessed with selected- or constructed-response items.

You may also use released items from the *Partnership for Assessment of Readiness for College and Careers* (PARCC). Access the following link below to access sample items and prototypes by grade level:

http://www.parcconline.org/samples/item-task-prototypes

Regarding item (iv), focus on your domain table and briefly map a conceptual development of your target content standard from the initial to the final phase. If applicable, consider as well the approach(es) noted in the CCSSM for that particular standard. For example, content standard 5.NF.7b provides three linked suggestions that will help students understand division of a whole number by a unit fraction (i.e.: beginning with a story context to motivate the definition, using a visual fraction model to determine quotient, and then drawing on the relationship between multiplication and division to explain why the answer makes sense).

Regarding item (v), briefly suggest instructional tools and activities that can help your students learn the articulated content and practice standards. For example, content standard 5.NF.7b can be taught by providing them with several different story problems of the same type and then letting them use number lines to make sense of division of whole numbers by unit fractions in terms of repeated subtraction. A template such as the one shown in Figure 10.3 can be used to help them process and convert their representations from story to visual to numerical forms.

Table 10.1 Initial Assessment-Learning-Teaching Plan

Group (names):	Grade Level: Class Type:		
Relevant standard for mathematical content Domain: Cluster: Standard:	Relevant standard for mathematical practices (check only one) General: _____ Make sense of problems and persevere in solving them _____ Reason abstractly and quantitatively _____ Construct viable arguments and critique the reasoning of others _____ Model with mathematics _____ Use appropriate tools strategically _____ Attend to precision _____ Look for and make use of structure _____ Look for and express regularity in repeated reasoning Specific:		
Evidence of attainment of content standard	Planned assessment item or task that will be used to establish evidence		
How students will learn the content and practice standards (a rough sketch of steps will suffice)	How the content and practice standards can be taught effectively (a rough sketch of steps will suffice)		

Story Problem:		
Division Expression	Number Line to Obtain Quotient	Check by Multiplication
Story Problem:		
Division Expression	Number Line to Obtain Quotient	Check by Multiplication

Figure 10.3. Template for division of whole numbers by unit fractions in compressed form

10.2 NORM- AND CRITERION-REFERENCED TESTS

One important concept in assessment involves norm- and criterion-referenced testing. In *norm-referenced testing* (NRT) an individual student's performance is compared to other students' performance on the same (valid and reliable) test. NRT results rank students on a curve, producing labels such as high and low achievers. Examples of NRTs are standardized assessments such as the Scholastic Aptitude Test and college entrance examinations. In *criterion-referenced testing* (CRT), an individual student's performance is assessed relative to some well-defined criteria or standards. CRT results tell whether the student has achieved mastery of a specific competence. Examples of CRT include the SBA, California's state-mandated assessment called Standardized Testing and Reporting (STAR), and the PARCC. In the case of the STAR program, an individual student's performance in mathematics is labeled either advanced (i.e., achieving beyond grade-level expectations), proficient (i.e., meeting grade-level expectations), basic (i.e., not meeting grade-level expectations), below basic, and far below basic. In California, "proficient" is the desired minimum achievement level for all students.

Work with a group and do the following tasks below.

a. Access the following two links below and discuss advantages and disadvantages of NRT and CRT. Can one test be used for two different purposes? Explain.

http://www.fairtest.org/criterion-and-standards-referenced-tests
http://www.cshe.unimelb.edu.au/assessinglearning/06/normvcrit6.html

b. Access the following link below and discuss the different kinds of scores that are generated by NRTs and CRTs and how they are interpreted.

http://www.cal.org/twi/evaltoolkit/5when2usetests.htm

c. Access the following link below and discuss item characteristics of NRT and CRT.

http://www.edpsycinteractive.org/topics/measeval/crnmref.html

10.3 PRINCIPLES OF EFFECTIVE CLASSROOM ASSESSMENTS

Access the following link below and answer the questions that follow.

http://www.ets.org/Media/Tests/TOEFL_Institutional_Testing_Program/ELLM2002.pdf

a. How are classroom assessments generally helpful to teachers?
b. When is an assessment considered to be valid and reliable, and why should such characteristics matter?
c. What are some suggestions for planning, writing, and implementing good assessments?
d. How do you prepare students to value classroom and other school-based assessments? What should they know before and after taking an assessment?

10.4 FORMATIVE ASSESSMENTS

Obtain a copy of the following article below by Greg Conderman and Laura Hedin on the nature and practice of formative assessments. Then work with a group to discuss the questions that follow.

Conderman, Greg and Hedin, Laura. (2012). Classroom assessments that inform instruction. *Kappa Delta Pi Record*, *48*, 162–168.

a. What are formative assessments (also called *adaptive instruction*)? How do they differ from summative assessments?
b. Describe formative assessment strategies that can be used before, during, and after instruction. What findings are pertinent at every phase, and how can they be effectively processed in class?
c. Identify a CCSSM domain, a cluster, and one content standard in the cluster. Identify one CCSSM practice standard that can be assessed with the content standard. Develop at least one formative assessment task before, during, and after a 55-minute classroom session.

10.5 SUMMATIVE ASSESSMENTS

This section provides you with an opportunity to learn the SBA system in detail. You may find the PARCC system interesting to learn as well. In case you study both summative assessment tools, determine similarities, differences, and essential components.

10.5.1 General Conceptions Surrounding Summative Assessments

Access the link below to read the perspective of Ezekiel Dixon-Roman regarding the role of formative and summative assessments in informing teaching and learning.

http://www.gordoncommission.org/rsc/pdfs/vol_1_no_2_18654.pdf

a. What are summative assessments? How do they differ from formative assessments? What does the author mean when he claims that both formative and summative assessments have a dynamic relationship? How can summative assessments be embedded in formative assessments?

b. Describe different types of summative assessment strategies and their purposes.

10.5.2 The Smarter Balanced Assessment (SBA)

Access the link below to download several key PowerPoint modules that will help you understand the SBA system.

http://www.smarterbalanced.org/smarter-balanced-assessments/item-writing-and-review/

Choose *Item Writing and Review* under the *Smarter Balanced Assessments* tab. Download the PowerPoint module labeled *Introduction to Smarter Balanced Item and Performance Task Development.* Provide responses to the questions below.

a. What is the SBA? What is the goal of the SBA Consortium? What are the basic key features of the SBA system?

b. Slide 9 describes the SBA item development process. For our purpose, focus only on steps 1 and 2. Briefly describe the evidence-centered design (i.e., assessment triangle) that guides each step in the process.

c. How are content and item specifications useful in the development of SBA items and tasks?

d. Learn the following SBA item ad task types below and their different purposes.
   i. selected response items;
   ii. constructed response items;
   iii. extended response items;
   iv. performance tasks;
   v. and technology-rich items (i.e., technology-enabled and technology-enhanced).

e. Describe important terms and key concepts that are central to understanding the SBA system.

Download the PowerPoint module labeled *Mathematics Selected Response, Constructed Response, and Technology-Enhanced Items*. This module provides an in-depth discussion of three of the four SBA item and task types, including guidelines and requirements for developing and writing such items. Provide responses to the following questions below.

  f. What are selected response items? What are the benefits and limitations of using such items? How are stems and distractors in traditional selected response items developed? What is the purpose of a distractor analysis? How are stimuli and stems in nontraditional selected response items developed? What is the purpose of a scoring rubric? Jump to slide 15 to learn about the qualities of a rubric. What are some basic guidelines for writing nontraditional selected response items?
  g. What are constructed response items? How are stimuli and stems in constructed response items developed? What is the purpose of a scoring rubric? What are some basic guidelines for developing constructed response items?
  h. What are some general guidelines and requirements for developing exemplary selected and constructed response items? What can be learned from the flawed items?
  i. What are technology-enabled items? How are they constructed?
  j. What are technology-enhanced items? How are they constructed? What are the key components in a technology-enhanced item? How are interaction spaces and scoring rules constructed? Study the template for creating technology-enhanced items.
  k. Explain similarities and differences between technology-enabled, technology-enhanced, and paper-based items.

Access the link below, which provides information on how to develop and write good performance tasks. Provide responses to the questions that follow.

  http://www.oakland.k12.mi.us/LinkClick.aspx?link=Learning%2FDRAFT+Performance+Task+Specifications_022812.pdf&tabid=1876&mid=7256

  l. What are the characteristics of good performance tasks?
  m. How are SBA performance tasks in mathematics constructed and administered in classrooms? How are they scored? How are rubrics constructed?
  n. Refer to pp. 15-17 for details regarding the structure of a performance task in mathematics. Access the following link below to investigate the Grade 4 sample performance task called Planting Tulips. Solve the task and evaluate the task specification and scoring rubric that came with the sample.

  http://www.smarterbalanced.org/sample-items-and-performance-tasks/

Download the PowerPoint module labeled *Mathematics Grade Level Considerations for Grades 3-5*. This module provides information regarding item and task development and content specification issues that apply to grades 3 through 5. Provide responses to the following questions below.

o. What are some basic suggestions regarding vocabulary, style, numbers, words, use of commas in numbers, representation of missing values, and contexts that are appropriate for grades 3 to 5 students?

p. SBA items and tasks are categorized not only by type but also by content specification. Content specification consists of four foundational claims and their respective assessment targets. Describe each claim, the relevant assessment targets, and item and task types that can be used to collect evidence. How are the CCSSM clusters used in Claim 1? How are the CCSSM practice standards used in Claims 2 through 4? Note that a student's Claim 1 score represents 40% of his or her total SBA math score, while the three remaining claims factor in 20% each.

Download the PowerPoint module labeled *Mathematics Content Specifications, Item Specifications, and Depth of Knowledge.* Pay careful attention to the cognitive rigor matrix that is used to develop high-quality items and tasks that are framed around the four foundational claims and their respective assessment targets. Provide responses to the following questions below.

q. What is the basis for SBA's cognitive rigor matrix?

r. How are elementary students assessed based on the four levels of depth of knowledge?

s. Explore the cognitive rigor matrix shown in slide 12. How does information from the table assist in the development of different levels of items and tasks?

t. The table shown in slide 15 identifies the number of assessment targets for Claim 1 under each grade level. Verify that each count is correct by inspecting the appropriate reference in the CCSSM document. For instance, p. 22 of the CCSSM contains 11 clusters of content standards that correspond to Claim 1 assessment targets for third grade.

u. Carefully investigate the structure of the sample Claim 1 assessment target shown in slide 16. How are headings and full description constructed? Focus on the assessment description and the notations that you see on the first line. Refer to pp. 29-39 and 79-81 of the following document below for more details regarding the different cluster emphases (i.e., major, additional, and supporting). Note that only major Claim 1 clusters are assessed in the SBA.

http://www.smarterbalanced.org/wordpress/wp-content/uploads/2011/12/Math-Content-Specifications.pdf

v. Assessment targets for Claims 2, 3, and 4 are drawn from the CCSSM practice standards and, hence, they are not grade-level specific. Notice that the targets under each claim should be similar to your Table 2.3 checklist of specific actions. Carefully investigate the structure of each set of assessment targets shown in slides 32 through 34. Which practice standards are assessed in Claim 2? 3? 4? Refer to pp. 55–78 of the document in (u) for more details.

w. Carefully investigate the structure of the sample item specification table shown in slide 36. See to it that you understand every component in the structure.

x. What is an evidence statement? How was the sample evidence statement shown in slide 37 constructed?

y. What is a task model? How were the sample task models shown in slide 38 constructed?

z. Slide 39 shows a sample of a SBA item that consists of multiple claims and assessment targets. How are such items processed?

Download the PowerPoint module labeled *Mathematics Stimulus Considerations*, which provides information regarding the purpose, types, and guidelines for developing and using stimuli in nontraditional selected and constructed response items.

aa. What are the different parts of a nontraditional selected or constructed response item?

bb. What are some suggestions for developing appropriate stimuli material?

Access the link below and refer to pp. 12 to 14 of the document, which list additional suggestions for developing, writing, and implementing classroom-based performance tasks and selected response items. Provide responses to the question that follow.

http://www.ets.org/Media/Tests/TOEFL_Institutional_Testing_Program/ELLM2002.pdf

cc. What should teachers do before and after administering a performance task?

dd. Which among the tips for writing good selected response items appear new to you?

10.6 PROJECTS AND PORTFOLIOS AS ALTERNATIVE SUMMATIVE ASSESSMENTS

Performance tasks provide one instance of projects. In this section you will learn about different kinds of projects, including portfolios. Access the following link below and answer the questions that follow.

http://www.intel.com/content/www/us/en/education/k12/project-design/design.html

a. What are projects? How are they different from worksheets in terms of purpose, scope of work, level of engagement, etc.?

b. What are some characteristics of good and well-defined projects? Investigate the sample project units for elementary K-2 and 3-5. What information should be included in a project unit?

c. What are the benefits of project-based learning? How does it support and enrich traditional classrooms? What do you need to consider in order for students to experience success in accomplishing project plans and goals? Access the link *Project in Action* for more information about changes in instruction as a result of implementing effective project-based learning in class.

d. What are some misconceptions related to project-based learning?

e. Open the file labeled *Plan a Project*. Learn the basic planning components and determine how they can be aligned with the structural components of the CCSSM and SBA.

f. Open the file labeled *Project Rubric*. How are projects assessed and graded?

Scoring rubrics are used to evaluate projects. They are either analytic or holistic in structure and content. Access the following links below to learn the differences between the two types in terms of purpose, advantages and disadvantages, development and design, guidelines, and scoring practices.

http://www.heinemann.com/shared/onlineresources/e00278/chapter4.pdf

http://www.uni.edu/chfasoa/analyticholisticrubrics.pdf

http://www.teachervision.fen.com/teaching-methods-and-management/rubrics/4524.html

https://resources.oncourse.iu.edu/access/content/user/mikuleck/Filemanager_Public_Files/EFL_Assessment/Unit_3/Metler_Designing_scoring_rubrics_for_your_classroom.pdf

Portfolios are collections of students' work that showcase their efforts, progress, and achievements within a given timeframe. Access the following links below to learn about traditional and electronic portfolios, including essential components, samples, and scoring guidelines.

http://www.gallaudet.edu/clerc_center/information_and_resources/info_to_go/transition_to_adulthood/portfolios_for_student_growth.html#MiddleRubrics

http://www.educationworld.com/a_tech/tech/tech111.shtml

10.7 MATH JOURNALS AND LESSON INVESTIGATIONS AS ALTERNATIVE FORMATIVE ASSESSMENTS

Some teachers use math journals in a formative context. Math journal writing should encourage elementary students to reflect and communicate their ideas and, in some cases, dispositions.

a. Access the following link below to learn about different journal writing strategies that apply in school mathematical contexts.

http://www.mcrel.org/~/media/Files/McREL/Homepage/Products/01_99/prod19_Writing_in_math.ashx

Discuss advantages of and potential issues with each strategy.

b. Access the following link below, which provides additional strategies for embedding writing in instruction and learning.

http://www-tc.pbs.org/teacherline/courses/rdla230/docs/session_1_burns.pdf

Which strategies look familiar? Which ones are new?

c. Access the following link below, which provides samples of math prompts about attitudes and dispositions.

http://www.readwritethink.org/files/resources/lesson_images/lesson820/MathPrompts.pdf

Generate short samples of math prompts that specifically address the practice standards.

Lesson investigations are short mini-projects or hands-on activities that students usually accomplish in one classroom session. For example, first-grade students who accomplish Activity Sheets 2.1 and 2.2 are provided with an opportunity to find patterns and develop a structure for generating addition facts in their own way. Effective math investigations enable them to explore and construct ideas, collect data, and perform experiments that begin informally and/or creatively. There is no prescribed mathematical method since they are meant to encourage students to use sense-making or adaptive strategies and problem-solving techniques. Through purposeful scaffolding from others, students begin to develop formal knowledge. Eventually, results in a math investigation yield correct and valid mathematical understandings that support the development of structures and routine knowledge. They also become the basis for more formal learning and instruction. Evaluation can be either holistic or analytic. Access the following link below for samples, guidelines, and a template.

http://montclairgifteded.wikispaces.com/file/view/Math+Investigation+Handout.doc

10.8 AN ASSESSMENT PROJECT

In this section, you will develop assessment items and tasks and provide details that draw on the SBA structure. Access the link below, which directs you to the SBA mathematics sample items and performance tasks page.

http://sampleitems.smarterbalanced.org/itempreview/sbac/index.htm

Click on the tab that says "View More Mathematics Sample Items." The table shows grade bands, the four foundational claims, and performance tasks.

Open the sample item labeled Fractions 1 (item 43044) that evaluates a Claim 1 assessment target. Click on the tab that says "About This Item." For the given selected response item, the following summary specification has been provided: (1) item name; (2) grade level; (3) claim; (4) target assessment; (5) CCSSM content standard; and (6) a brief description of the task in the form of an evidence statement and the relevant task model.

Open the sample item labeled Rectangle 1 (item 43022) that evaluates a Claim 2 assessment target. For this particular constructed response item, the "About This Item" specification addresses the above 6 components and an analytic rubric (why?).

Open the sample item labeled *Planting Tulips*, which is a performance task that seeks to evaluate eight assessment target claims. The following specification for the item addresses the following components: (1) classroom activity; (2) student task; (3) task specifications; and (4) a detailed analytic scoring rubric (why?).

Do the following tasks below.

a. Identify a grade level and a CCSSM domain and develop five SBA-type items and tasks. One assessment item should be a performance task, and the remaining four items should assess four different claims. Open the link below for more detailed samples of items under each claim.

http://www.smarterbalanced.org/wordpress/wp-content/uploads/2011/12/Math-Content-Specifications.pdf

b. Be sure to provide an item distractor analysis in the case of selected response items. Also, develop scoring rubrics on all constructed response items and performance tasks.

c. See to it that every assessment item that you develop comes with an "About This Item" specification. Also, the performance task you construct should follow the same structure provided in the case of the *Planting Tulips* sample.

d. Make sure that all items and tasks are assessed based on in the cognitive rigor matrix.

CONTENT-PRACTICE LEARNING

In this chapter you will deal with issues relevant to elementary students' content-practice learning of mathematics. In section 11.1, you will establish and articulate a general definition of learning that will help guide the manner in which you expect your students to learn the CCSSM. In section 11.2, you will explore one historical interpretation of the complex relationship between learning theories and the US school mathematics curriculum through the years, which will help you understand various contentious issues and concerns in mathematics education. In section 11.3, you will learn relevant issues surrounding the *Math War* and possible consequences when you hold extreme or narrow views of learning school mathematical knowledge. In section 11.4, you will further deepen your understanding of the theories of Piaget and Vygotsky as they relate to mathematics learning and Fuson's middle-ground perspective – learning-path developmentally appropriate learning/teaching model –that emphasizes growth in elementary students' understanding and fluency of mathematics. To fully appreciate Fuson's learning model, you will explore the notion of a learning progression (LP) in some detail in section 11.5. LPs are useful to know for other reasons. The evidence and research that were used to support the content structure of the CCSSM significantly drew on LPs. You will also use LPs in Chapter 12 on content-practice teaching when you develop and write your unit and lesson plans. In section 11.6, which closes this chapter, you will learn current issues and concerns involving brain-based studies and their implications to elementary students' learning of mathematics.

11.1 DEFINING LEARNING

Access the first-grade classroom video *Leprechaun Traps* from the link below. Watch the first three minutes of the video and answer the questions that follow.

https://www.teachingchannel.org/videos?page=2&categories=subjects_ math,organizations_national&load=2

a. Which Common Core State content and practice standards in mathematics did the students exhibit in this short segment of the video? Refer to p. 4 of the CCSSM for a description of *mathematical understanding*. Assess the extent to which the students mathematically understood the number tasks that they processed together in class.

b. The students in Ms. Jeanne Wright's class also exhibited learning. Search the internet for at least ten definitions of learning to help you construct a *Learning wordle*. Which terms appear prominently in your wordle? Formulate a definition of learning based on your wordle.

c. Access the article below, which discusses several different meanings of learning.

De Houwever, Jan, Barnes-Holmes, Dermot, and Moors, Agnes. (2013). What is learning? *Psychon Bull Rev*, 20, 631-642.

Compare the definition of learning that you developed in (b) with the authors' functional definition of learning. Which components in the authors' definition of learning are reflected in your own definition? Which ones are different? Which ones are not mentioned? Which ones appear to be essential? Do you agree with their definition of learning? How is growth in mathematical understanding accounted for in such definitions of learning?

d. At this stage you should have developed a well-conceptualized view of learning. Think about the first-grade students in Ms. Wright's class and assess how they learned in her class. What did they actually learn from the number combinations activity?

11.2 CHANGING VIEWS OF LEARNING AND THEIR EFFECTS IN THE ELEMENTARY MATHEMATICS CURRICULUM

Access the following article below, which provides an interesting historical analysis of factors that contributed to cycles of change in the US school mathematics curriculum. Answer the questions that follow.

Lambdin, Diana and Walcott, Crystal. (2007). Changes through the years: Connections between psychological learning theories and the school mathematics curriculum. *NCTM 69th Yearbook*. Reston, VA: NCTM.

a. Read the narrative provided under **each** phase in the history of the school mathematics curriculum and then address the following questions related to learning:

i. Describe the social conditions that motivated the change in teaching practice and assessment of student learning.

ii. Use De Houwever, Barnes-Holmes, and Moors's three components of learning to assess how students were expected to learn and understand mathematics.

ii. Explore how content-practice learning might have taken shape in math classrooms.

b. Describe shared, different, and, more importantly, essential views of learning across the six phases.

c. Consider your own recent experiences in the classroom. Pay special attention to how you learned mathematics. Are there concerns, issues, or other factors relevant to your own learning experiences that have not been addressed in the article and are worth noting?

11.3 MATH WARS: DEBATING ABOUT WHAT AND HOW STUDENTS SHOULD LEARN MATHEMATICS

Go back to the first-grade classroom video *Leprechaun Traps* and watch how the students dealt with the story problem that had them forming combinations of numbers for the whole number 30. Then access the following two articles below, which provide detailed commentaries regarding the *Math War* in the history of US school mathematics education. Answer the questions that follow.

Schoenfeld, Alan. (2004). The math wars. *Educational Policy*, 18(1), 253-286.

Crary, Alice and Wilson, Stephen. (2013). The faulty logic of the "math wars." *The New York Times Opinionator*.

a. What motivated the Math War between traditionalists and reformists? Describe issues and concerns raised by each camp and determine whether they make sense to you.
b. How might each camp analyze the manner in which the first-grade students in Ms. Wright's class exhibited their learning of number combinations from the initial problem solving phase to the final whole-group discussion phase? What concerns might each camp have before, during, and after the implementation of the *Leprechaun Trap* task?
c. Another unfortunate consequence that emerged from the Math War involves making a distinction between routine knowledge and flexible or adaptive knowledge. Learning that yields routine knowledge exhibits understanding and correct application of simple, complex, and sophisticated routines in efficient ways. Learning that yields adaptive knowledge exhibits some level of routine competence, but there is also an acquired disposition towards inventing strategies and thinking about solutions in different ways. Assess the video for instances of routine and flexible knowledge.
d. Is there a way out of the Math War? What can you learn from this unfortunate event in the history of US school mathematics education?

11.4 UNDERSTANDING PIAGETIAN AND VYGOTSKIAN VIEWS OF LEARNING IN MATHEMATICS AND FINDING A WAY OUT OF EXTREME VIEWS OF LEARNING

In this section, you will further deepen your understanding of Piagetian and Vygotskian views in relation to children's learning of mathematics. Access the following article below and read the first six pages. Answer the questions that follow.

Fuson, Karen. (2009). Avoiding misinterpretations of Piaget and Vygotsky: Mathematical teaching without learning, learning without teaching, or helpful learning-path teaching? *Cognitive Development*, 24, 343-348.

a. How are elementary students expected to learn mathematics in a Piagetian context? What are some unfortunate consequences of misinterpreting mathematics learning in this context?
b. How is mathematical learning expected to occur in a Vygotskian context? Compare your answers to your findings in (a). What are some unfortunate consequences of misinterpreting mathematics learning in a Vygotskian context?
c. Fuson recommends a balanced learning-teaching path model as a way out of extreme misreadings of Piaget and Vygotsky. How are students expected to learn mathematics in Fuson's context? Go back to the first-grade classroom video and assess the extent to which Ms. Wright modeled the different components of the balanced learning-teaching model listed under Table 2 on p. 347 of the article.

11.5 LEARNING PROGRESSIONS IN SCHOOL MATHEMATICS

You have come across the term *learning progressions* (LPs) several times in the preceding chapters and in various references from articles you have read. As you know, the content standards in the CCSSM have been carefully informed by LPs. Consequently, constructing lesson plans and activities in the mathematics classroom involves developing appropriate learning paths that are informed by LPs. Access the following links below to learn more about LPs in mathematics and answer the questions that follow.

http://www.cpre.org/sites/default/files/researchreport/1220_learningtrajectories inmathcciireport.pdf

https://www.mheonline.com/assets/pdf/program/building_blocks_learning_ trajectories.pdf

a. What are LPs? How are they similar to and different from learning trajectories? How are they similar to and different from typical scope-and-sequence planning activities? What are the essential characteristics in a LP?
b. What should you be concerned about regarding LPs in school mathematics?
c. How can LPs be used to inform content-practice teaching and assessment?

The following site below contains links to six detailed LPs involving the major content domains that comprise the K-5 CCSSM. Work with a group of four students and explore a specific LP together. Follow the instructions below.

http://ime.math.arizona.edu/progressions

d. Read the LP for the domain. Assess the logic and reasonableness of the proposed progression. Discuss possible benefits to students in the long term, including potential issues and concerns.

e. All elementary teachers prepare well for the for *Back to School Night*. A nerve-wracking part of the meeting involves presenting to parents, administrators, and colleagues information about each curriculum that matters to students and instructional activities or methods that will be used to help them achieve the relevant learning goals. Develop a LP poster for your domain. Construct either a map or a path and present details about your LP in a format that is interesting and sensible. Access any of the following links below, which provide initial sources of information about making posters.

http://abacus.bates.edu/~bpfohl/posters/#titles (Creating a Poster in PowerPoint)

http://clt.lse.ac.uk/poster-design/ (Poster Design Tips)

http://www.iris.edu/hq/files/programs/education_and_outreach/poster_pilot/Poster_Guide_v2a.pdf (Pedagogical Power of Posters and Tips)

11.6 LEARNING FROM NEUROSCIENCE

Recent discussions on learning in schools recommend the use of brain-based interventions that depend on valid neuroscientific evidence. In this section, you will learn about the nature of such evidence and, especially, the manner in which results need to be interpreted in light of the constraints in studies that generated them. Access the following article below to learn about neuroscientific evidence and implications to elementary students' learning of mathematics. Answer the questions that follow.

Rivera, Ferdinand. (2012). Neural correlates of gender, culture, and race and implications to embodied thinking in mathematics. In H. Forgasz and F. Rivera (eds.), *Towards equity in mathematics education* (pp. 515-543). New York: Springer.

a. Distinguish between descriptive and prescriptive information in relation to neural mechanisms that support cognitive processes in mathematical thinking and learning. What does this mean in practical terms?

b. Neuroscience evidence is basically correlational and not causational in nature. Further, there is a difference between neural and psychological evidence. What do such types of evidence mean in relation to the teaching and learning of mathematics?

c. How is learning defined in neuroscientific terms? Discuss the different types of memory and their implications to cognitive processing.

d. Describe the four lobes that divide the human cerebral cortex and their individual functions.

e. What do you learn from Nieder's research regarding the neurobiological evolution of symbolic thinking and reasoning in humans and nonhuman primates?

f. Describe Dehaene's neural network of triple coding and its implications to mathematical learning.

g. What do you learn from neural studies that target mathematical, linguistic, and visuospatial processing?

h. What are some implications of neural studies that focus on gender, race, and culture to mathematics teaching, learning, and assessment at the elementary level?

CONTENT-PRACTICE TEACHING

In this chapter you will deal with content-practice issues relevant to teaching elementary school mathematics. You will explore different teaching models and write unit plans and lesson plans. The component of teaching completes the alignment mindset that you have been asked to frequently bear in mind in your developing professional understanding of teaching to the CCSSM. That is, as indicated in Figure 12.1, issues on content-practice teaching are also about issues on content-practice learning and assessment. The pedagogical troika shapes the manner in which the CCSSM is implemented in individual classrooms.

12.1 DESCRIBING (GOOD) TEACHING

Access the fifth-grade classroom video *A Passion for Fractions* from the link below. As you watch the 13-minute video, answer the questions that follow. Work with a group and deal with the questions together.

https://www.teachingchannel.org/videos?page=2&categories=subjects_math,organizations_national&load=2

a. Identify the Common Core State content and practice standards in mathematics that the fifth-grade teacher, Ms. Betty Pittard, wanted her students to learn relative to the day's lesson. Pay special attention on the CCSSM-suggested mathematical strategies for processing the content.

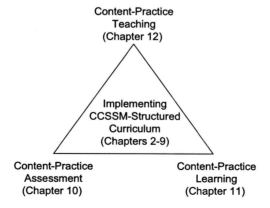

Figure 12.1. Grounding a CCSSM-structured curriculum around the pedagogical troika

b. Use the peer classroom observation tool shown in Table 12.1 to help you gather information about key content-practice events that transpired in Ms. Pittard's class. *A content-practice event* pertains to a teaching/learning episode where a teacher is explicitly modeling a particular practice-based action as a way of supporting his or her students understand a target content standard. For each key content-practice event in Ms. Pittard's class, assess the quality of the questions she used in terms of the cognitive rigor matrix you learned in Chapter 10.

c. What do you learn from Ms. Pittard's classroom session about what it means for teachers to teach to the CCSSM?

Access the following article below, which describes general characteristics of (good) teaching. Answer the questions that follow.

Tell, Carol. (2001). Appreciating good teaching: A conversation with Lee Shulman. *Educational Leadership*, 6–11.

d. How does Lee Shulman describe (good) teaching?

e. To what extent does Ms. Pittard's teaching style model the characteristics you identified in (d)?

Access the following article below, which describes three important activities that encourage students to engage in meaningful mathematical activity in the classroom. Answer the questions that follow.

Fisher, Douglas, Frey, Nancy, and Anderson, Heather. (2011). Thinking and comprehending in the mathematics classroom. In M. Pitici and F. Dyson (eds.), *The best writing on mathematics* (pp. 188–202). New Jersey: Princeton University Press.

f. The authors provided an example of a typical teaching episode in a 9th-grade mathematics class. Describe the teacher's instruction and identify possible consequences on content-practice assessment and learning.

g. The authors identified modeling, vocabulary development, and productive group work as three effective instructional strategies for engaging students in the mathematics classroom. How does each strategy support good content-practice learning? Re-evaluate Ms. Pittard's teaching style based on these strategies.

12.2 TEACHING MODELS IN ELEMENTARY SCHOOL MATHEMATICS SETTINGS

In this section, you will explore six models of teaching mathematics that are appropriate at the elementary level. It should be noted that while the models are discussed separately, effective teaching often involves employing combinations of two or more models. As you learn more about each model and its components, consider how content-practice strategies can be integrated into the components.

Table 12.1. Peer classroom observation tool

Peer Classroom Observation for _____ (Name of Teacher)	Grade Level and Class Type: _____					
CCSSM Content Standard/s	CCSSM Practice Standard/s					
Domain: Cluster: Standard/s:	Cluster: Specific Actions:					
Sequence of Key Content-Practice Events and Relevant Materials Used	Supportive Questions Used to Facilitate the Event	Cognitive Rigor Analysis (Depth of knowledge and type of thinking exhibited by students)				

12.2.1 E-I-S-Driven Teaching

The acronym E-I-S stands for Jerome Bruner's three modes of representation, *Enactive-Iconic-Symbolic*. When you introduce elementary students to representations in school mathematics for the first time, a good entry point involves providing them with opportunities to act on objects that represent a target knowledge (enactive). Hopefully over instructional time, they will learn to think about such representations mentally (iconic) and linguistically (symbolic). Language in the symbolic phase is the domain of codes in contracted or condensed forms, generalizations, and abstractions. In the symbolic phase, students overcome limitations in enactive- and iconic-based representations. Work with a group and do the following two tasks below.

    a. Search the internet for more discussions regarding the E-I-S progression. Provide detailed characteristics of each type of representation and activities that support them. Discuss advantages and disadvantages of each type. Should E-I-S be taught in that order?

    b. Identify a CCSSM content-practice standard and illustrate how it can be taught in an E-I-S manner.

12.2.2 C-R-A Sequenced Teaching

The acronym C-R-A stands for *Concrete-Representational-Abstract*. C-R-A sequenced teaching emerged from intervention studies involving students with learning difficulties. Both the C-R-A and E-I-S models share common features such as using various multisensory techniques (i.e., visual, auditory, kinesthetic, and tactile strategies) that support students' thinking in the abstract phase of learning. But the R in C-R-A involves much more than the I in E-I-S in the sense that students are encouraged to draw pictures as a way of helping them transition to the abstract phase. In school mathematical contexts, meaningful and effectively drawn pictures are *diagrammatic* in nature. That is, they reflect schemes or patterns that convey necessary mathematical relationships. Hence, constructed diagrams on problem solving tasks are not mere pictures or faithful copies of objects. You may want to think about the math drawings shown in sections 6.1 and 6.6. While such diagrams initially emerged from pictures that resembled the Dienes blocks, the simplified versions emphasized the underlying mathematical relationships.

    c. Continue working with the same group and address the same two tasks listed in 12.2.1 relative to the C-R-A teaching model.

12.2.3 Van Hiele Sequenced Teaching

The van Hiele sequenced teaching involves the following five phases of geometrical thinking: visual; analysis; abstraction; deduction; and rigor. The model initially geometrical emerged from the research studies of Dina van Hiele-Geldof and Pierre van Hiele in relation to students' thinking about school geometric concepts. Think about your learning experiences in Chapter 8. Hopefully the different sections have encouraged you to progress in your gometrical thinking from the visual phase (recognizing and sorting objects based on surface appearances) to the analysis phase (developing initial properties about objects) and the abstract phase (constructing definitions based on common properties of a set of objects and making sense of inclusive relationships). The deductive and rigor phases involve formal mathematical reasoning and systems thinking, skills that students learn in high school geometry and beyond.

d. Keep working with the same group and address the same two tasks listed in 12.2.1 relative to the van Hiele teaching model.

12.2.3 Culturally-Relevant Teaching

Culturally-relevant teaching emerged from the work of Gloria Ladson-Billings, which involves employing culturally-responsive instructional strategies and activities. That is, one way of teaching mathematics in a meaningful manner involves adapting instruction and developing activities that draw on students' culture, which exerts a significant influence in the way they think and learn. Effective culturally-responsive contexts motivate them to participate in class and develop a productive mathematical disposition. Continue working with your group and address the following four tasks below.

e. Conduct an internet search that provides reliable information about the race and ethnic profiles of students in today's mathematics classrooms.
f. Search the internet for more discussions regarding culturally-relevant teaching. What conceptions and misconceptions do you need to know about this teaching approach?
g. Describe a few general instructional strategies or activities that either draw on cultural referents or model cultural relevance. Use at least one of them to help you teach the content-practice standard you identified in (b) in a culturally responsive manner.
h. Drawing on students' *funds of knowledge* is a related culturally-responsive perspective that, according to Luis Moll, Cathy Amanti, Deborah Neff, and Norma Gonzalez, "refers to the historically accumulated and culturally developed bodies of knowledge and skills essential for household or individual functioning and well-being." Search the internet for discussions regarding this perspective and ways in which mathematics teachers have used them to inform their own instruction and pedagogical practices.

12.2.4 SDAIE-Driven Teaching

The acronym SDAIE stands for *Specially Designed Academic Instruction in English*. A SDAIE-driven teaching approach targets the needs of English learners who need appropriate scaffolding or "comprehensible input" to help them obtain full and equal access to academic concepts and language. Continue working with the same group and address the two tasks below.

i. Who is an *English learner* (EL)? Access the following link below for a good overview of this concept from the Council of Chief State School Officers. Pay attention on key factors that you need to know about ELs.

http://www.ccsso.org/Documents/2013/Toward_a_Common_Definition_2013.pdf?utm_source=buffer&utm_campaign=Buffer&utm_content=buffer3f9b6&utm_medium=twitter

j. Address the same tasks described in (f) and (g) in 12.2.3 but with the SDAIE teaching model in mind.

12.2.5 Differentiated Instruction

Differentiated instruction is a teaching model that employs a variety of instructional strategies as a way of adapting to the different needs of individual learners in a classroom. Effective teachers who exhibit this teaching model design their curricular and classroom activities in ways that enable *all* their students to achieve the same standards and proficiency levels despite (initial) differences in cognitive processing ability. Such differences stem from a variety of factors such as readiness level, learning profile, interests, etc.

k. Continue working with the same group and address tasks (f) and (g) in relative to the differentiated instruction model.
l. Access the following link below that illustrates how second-grade teacher Mr. Pronovost employs differentiated instruction in helping his students learn addition and subtraction based on their current proficiency levels.

https://www.teachingchannel.org/videos/differentiating-in-math?utm_source=Teaching+Channel+Newsletter&utm_campaign=66a9b38bed-Newsletter_September_28_2013&utm_medium=email&utm_term=0_23c3feb22a-66a9b38bed-291836021

m. How does Mr. Pronovost explicitly structure technology use in his classroom to help him achieve effective differentiated instruction? If your classroom does not have sufficient technology resources, how might you use your available classroom resources so that you yield the same " freedom to differentiate?"

12.2.6 Flip Teaching

Flip teaching is a teaching model that basically reverses classroom time for traditional instruction and homework time for practice. This model begins with the assumption that all students have open access to either a computer or the internet.

Teachers assign video lessons for them to study on their own (as a homework task), which often deal with introductory or basic information. Classroom time is then used to engage them in problem-solving activity that requires them to use higher-order thinking skills. Since flip teaching promotes blended learning in the sense just described, lecturing is almost minimized or even eliminated and is replaced by problem-solving activity. Continue working with the same group and address the following two tasks below.

n. Access the following link below to learn more about how this teaching model is used in particular schools. Generate a few initial impressions. Also, assess which among the teaching models in the preceding subsections are compatible with this particular model.

http://www.boston.com/bostonglobe/editorial_opinion/oped/articles/2011/09/18/flipping_for_math/

o. Deal with tasks (f) and (g) with the flip teaching model in mind.

12.3 TEACHING WITH CONCRETE AND VIRTUAL MANIPULATIVES, COMPUTER-BASED LEARNING TOOLS, AND VIDEO GAMES AND APPS

Manipulatives are objects that elementary teachers use to model concepts, ideas, and processes in school mathematics. For example, the Dienes blocks shown in Figure 2.4 represent concrete power-of-ten groupings that support students' mathematical understanding of whole number operations. Manipulatives such as fraction pieces drawn from the National Library of Virtual Manipulatives are virtual, online, and technology-enhanced versions of their concrete forms. Access the link below for samples of virtual manipulatives.

http://nlvm.usu.edu/en/nav/vlibrary.html

Access the following articles below, which address various aspects relevant to the nature and use of manipulatives in elementary classroom settings. Read them together first and then answer the questions that follow.

Clements, Douglas and McMillen, Sue. (1996). Rethinking "concrete" manipulatives. *Teaching Children Mathematics*, 2(5), 270–279.

Moyer, Patricia, Bolyard, Johnna, and Spikell, Mark. (2002). What are virtual manipulatives? *Teaching Children Mathematics*, 8(6), 372–377.

Puchner, Laurel, Taylor, Ann, O'Donnell, Barbara, and Fick, Kathleen. (2002). Teacher learning and mathematics manipulatives: A collective case study about teacher use of manipulatives in elementary and middle school mathematics lessons. *School Science and Mathematics*, 108(7), 313–325.

   a. How might you use manipulatives effectively in the mathematics classroom? Generate a list of dos and donts.

   b. Discuss the role of manipulatives in each teaching model in section 12.2.

All computer-based learning tools and video games and apps provide every student with an opportunity to (visually) engage in mathematical knowledge construction and development. They involve a good amount of interactive or dynamic experience, enabling students to generate abductions (i.e., formulate conjectures), perform inductions (i.e., repeatedly test conjectures), and experience deductive closure (i.e., apply rules to several more problems). They are intended to help students make progressive transitions in their conceptual understanding of a target content knowledge, skill, or application.

   c. Address the same tasks described in (f) and (g) in 12.2.3 but in the context of games and apps.

Access the following article below, which provides a good synthesis of research on the efficacy of teaching mathematics with concrete manipulatives.

Carbonneau, Kira, Marley, Scott, and Selig, James. (2013). A meta-analysis of the efficacy of teaching mathematics with concrete manipulatives. *Journal of Educational Psychology, 105*(2), 380–400.

   d. Revisit the list you constructed in (a) and compare your responses with the findings noted in the article. Add more to your list, if necessary.

   e. In previous sections you explored several different examples of games and apps that support students' learning of mathematics. To what extent do the authors' findings and recommendations relative to concrete manipulatives apply to games and apps?

12.4 TEACHING MATHEMATICS WITH GUIDE QUESTIONS

Regardless of teaching approach, asking the right questions when elementary students are engaged in content-practice learning is just as equally important as knowing when and how to use manipulatives in mathematical activity. Employing guide questions is a useful formative (i.e., ongoing) assessment technique that can be implemented before, during, and after instruction in either individual or group contexts. Guide questions set the mood and tone of content-practice learning in the classroom. In fact, they influence the direction of both the lesson and the depth or quality of students' learning experiences and content-practice driven knowledge.

One effective way of helping students develop a consistent mindset towards content-practice learning involves using appropriate guide questions that cue them to specific practice-based actions. Access Table 3 on pp. 14-16 from the link below for examples of good guide questions under each practice standard.

http://www.cde.ca.gov/ci/ma/cf/documents/aug2013overview1.
pdf#search=examples%20of%20questioning%20strategies%20teachers%20
might%20use%20to%20support%20mathematical%20176%20thinking%20
and%20stude&view=FitH&pagemode=none

Access the following three links below, which will provide you with an introduction to the nature of good questions, how they are created, what teachers need to do when posing good questions, and samples of possible generic and key questions to ask in a variety of contexts. Work with a group and answer the questions that follow.

http://www4.uwm.edu/org/mmp/PDFs/Yr5_PDFs/ThoughtProvokingQuestions-slides.pdf

http://www-tc.pbs.org/teachers/_files/pdf/TL_MathCard.pdf

http://www.fcps.org/cms/lib02/MD01000577/Centricity/Domain/97/The%20art%20of%20questioning%20in%20math%20class.pdf

a. Generate guide questions for each classroom situation presented on pages 6-7 of the third document.
b. Access Ms. Pittard's classroom video once again and reassess the type and quality of the guide questions that she used to help her fifth-grade students achieve the target content and practice standards relevant to the concept of multiplication involving two proper fractions.

12.5 CONTENT-PRACTICE UNIT PLANNING

Unit planning is one very exciting aspect of your job. Regardless of school or district context and resources, you will always need to plan a unit to help you write sensible, coherent, and logical lesson plans. The unit-planning process can be accomplished either individually, which rarely happens these days, or collectively with grade- or subject-level colleagues. Research on effective mathematics departments indicates that teachers who plan units, lessons, and assessments together produce much better results in student learning than teachers who prefer to plan alone. However, for the purpose of this section and considering the fact that you are learning to teach mathematics, you will need to develop your own unit plans in order to experience firsthand what this process entails. Also, since feedback matters, you will need to share your unit plan with a group and critique each other's work. In schools, inservice teachers often rely on feedback from other individuals (e.g.: grade-level teammates; math coach; subject-matter coordinator; principal), so you need to get used to it.

Content-practice unit planning (CPUP) involves developing, managing, and assessing a sequence of related content-practice lesson plans that is implemented within a stipulated range of time. The given description involves the following three important aspects of CPUP.

- There is a content-practice lesson sequence to be developed, taught, and assessed.
- Content-practice lessons are related in some way.
- Considering the preparation and time needed for planning, the implementation phase requires at least one work week.

There is no scientific basis for the minimum and maximum number of sessions that comprise a CPUP. However, in practical terms, really long CPUPs (say, one month) can be difficult to achieve. While the ultimate decision rests on you (or your group), it is important to obtain feedback at all times. Another very important factor in your decision-making process involves how well you know your grade-level content-practice standards. Other factors that are worth considering pertain to various psychological and institutional constraints that affect instructional delivery and time. Examples include the following: accounting for students' needs; demographic information; learning profiles of students in your class, grade level, school, and district; grade-level planning with colleagues; district-mandated pacing guides and periodic benchmark assessment issues; and school- and district-wide extracurricular activities and affairs.

Developing a coherent and well-articulated CPUP involves addressing the thirteen content-practice related tasks listed in Table 12.2. Taken together, they target *left-foot* unit planning. *Right-foot* unit planning takes into account all the intended and unintended psychological and institutional constraints that shape and complicate the daily task of teaching. Hence, a successful unit-walk orchestration, which is a perennial task for all novice and experienced teachers, involves learning to smoothly coordinate between left- and right-foot requirements. Chapter 13 addresses right-foot planning concerns. In the remainder of this section, you will focus on left-foot CPUP issues.

When you begin CPUP, you need to define your *unit*. A mathematics curriculum can be structured as units in several different ways, as follows:

- Domain-driven units;
- Cluster-driven units;
- Content standard-driven units;
- Chapter-driven units;
- Pacing guide-driven units.

The first three structures reflect the CCSSM framework, while the fourth and fifth structures reflect textbook- and school- or district-mandated structures, respectively. Regardless of the type of unit structure, however, both the CCSSM content-practice standards and SBA (or PARCC) need to be embedded in all the lessons.

As an example, refer to the mathematical content overview for second-grade students on p. 18 of the CCSSM. There are at least three ways of organizing the content overview by unit. If you choose to organize your units by domain, the *Operations and Algebraic Thinking (OAT)* as one unit will require more time to accomplish than the *Geometry* unit, which means you may need to break down the OAT domain into several smaller units. If you choose to organize your units by

Table 12.2. Content-Practice Unit Planning Steps

Pre-CPUP Concern

0. Obtaining first impressions of a target unit

Content-Practice Framing Concerns

1. Labeling the unit
2. Identifying primary (and, if applicable, secondary) big idea/s
3. Identifying key concepts and processes that are relevant to understanding the big idea/s
4. Developing specific essential questions for each concept and process
5. Developing a unit content overview, abstract, or summary
6. Producing a well-organized and well-justified unit content trajectory in the form of a concept map
7. Generating rough overviews or drafts of individual content-practice lesson plans that will accomplish each essential question identified in step (4).
8. Developing a content-practice unit assessment plan
9. Identifying prerequisite knowledge, skills, and content-practice standards

Content-Practice Implementation Concerns

10. Planning for effective time management
11. Identifying relevant materials and resources
12. Articulating accommodation-related issues and resources

---

cluster, then you will need to develop ten units since the content overview consists of ten clusters. To some extent, chapter-driven units are organized by cluster. If you choose to organize your units by content standard, you will need to develop twenty-six units. District- and school-developed pacing guides are often organized in several different ways, and grade-level teams usually work together to organize unit planning around such constraints. Work with a group and address the following task below.

   a. Search the internet for at least three samples of pacing guides and describe common, different, and essential components and/or structures.

To better understand the steps in Table 12.2, access the following link below, which provides you with a sample Grade 2 chapter drawn from the textbook, *Math Connects*, published by Macmillan and McGraw-Hill Glencoe. Consider the textbook chapter as your unit that consists of nine lessons. Continue working with the same group and respond to the following tasks below. Use the unit plan template shown in Table 12.3 to help you organize and record your responses.

   http://advancetracker.com/Advance_eBook/Main.html?bookId=760942

b. Step 0 involves obtaining first impressions of a target unit. Browse through the chapter, the different lessons, and the chapter exercises. Gather information about concepts and processes that all students need to learn by the end of the chapter. Check the CCSSM and determine the applicable domain, cluster, and content standards that map with the chapter. Assess the chapter's examples and tasks in terms of the examples and recommendations provided in the CCSSM, including sample SBA items that are available. Identify the relevant CCSSM practice standards that can be used to support and facilitate content knowledge acquisition.

c. Step 1 involves labeling the unit. Labeling enables you to convey in explicit terms the primary content knowledge (i.e., the topic) that you want your students to learn about the unit. Provide a label for this particular unit.

d. Step 2 involves identifying the primary and, if applicable, secondary big idea(s) for the unit. Randall Charles defines a big idea in mathematics in the following manner: "A *Big Idea* is a statement of an idea that is central to the learning of mathematics, one that links numerous mathematical understandings into a coherent whole." Provide a big idea statement for this particular unit. Limit to two sentences. Note that such a statement is not a complex outline of content and practice standards but simply a concise and clear expression of a synthesized mathematical idea that students will explore throughout the implementation phase.

e. Step 3 involves identifying key mathematical concepts and/processes that are relevant to understanding the big idea(s). The analysis involved in this step is still content-driven and does not have to be expressed in terms of content and practice standards. Regardless of standard, in fact, this step should help you identify content and academic language that need to be emphasized throughout the unit. List down all key concepts, processes, and/or academic language that are relevant to know for this particular unit.

f. Step 4 involves developing specific essential question(s) that will help you tackle your big idea(s). Following Grant Wiggins and Jay McTighe, an *essential question* expresses what students need to answer in order to say that they have learned, understood, and made sense of an aspect of the big idea. Once again, such questions do not need to depend on particular content-practice standards. Identify essential questions for this particular unit. Later, in step 6, you will be asked to map individual content-practice lesson plans with the relevant essential question(s).

g. Step 5 involves developing a unit content overview, abstract, or summary. This step requires you to reread your earlier responses in order to help you develop a coherent narrative of the unit that you can share with interested stakeholders (e.g., parents and colleagues). When you write your narrative description, you may begin to point out relationships between the unit and the relevant CCSSM content and practice standards, which convey your target learning outcomes for the unit. You may also want to point out the connections between and among the lessons in your unit and the relevant academic language that matter.

Highlight materials and resources that you intend to use as well. Develop an overview for this particular unit.

h. Step 6 involves producing a unit content trajectory in the form of a concept map. Generally, a *concept map* is a graphical representation that shows relationships between concepts in a unit. A *content trajectory* can be conveyed through a concept map, but the map should also reflect a (multi-)path sequence of concepts that models one plausible progressive emergence of content knowledge from the initial phase to the final phase. Your sequence of content-practice lesson plans is expected to draw on this analysis. Follow each step below to help you construct a content trajectory for this particular unit.

1. For each lesson in the chapter, identify key concepts and processes that students need to learn. Generate a label for each concept and/or process and then record the label in a post-it note.

2. Reassemble the labeled post-it notes that you developed for the entire unit in the form of a concept map. Check to make sure that your concept map reflects a well-reasoned and logical content trajectory, showing transitions in content knowledge from the simple and informal or beginning phase to the complex and sophisticated phase.

i. Steps 7 and 8 go together. These two steps involve mapping the content-driven analysis in the preceding steps with the relevant Common Core content and practice standards.

Step 7 involves generating rough drafts of lesson plans that will help you accomplish the different aspects of your unit. Table 12.4 provides a template for organizing lesson plan drafts. The primary intent in writing lesson plan drafts is to gather initial impressions of basic requirements that you will need to answer the target essential questions. The requirements for each essential question involve identifying: the applicable CCSSM content and practice standards; activities, materials, and resources that will help you teach the lesson; the appropriate formative and summative assessment tasks that will help you evaluate learning and instruction; and the amount of time that your students will need to answer the essential question. See to it that you take into account both instructional days and additional time for assessment and reteaching days when you determine the total number of sessions you need to accomplish a lesson.

Step 8 involves developing a unit assessment plan, which includes information about formative and summative assessment tasks that you intend to use to evaluate your students' understanding of the unit. Following the SBA style that you learned in Chapter 10, label each task for easy referencing. Use Table 12.5 to help you assess your tasks in terms of their alignment with the CCSSM content and practice standards. Use Table 12.6 to help you assess your tasks according to their levels of cognitive rigor (see section 10.5.2 item (u) for details regarding the cognitive rigor matrix).

Develop an assessment plan for this unit. Make sure that you clearly provide a label for each assessment task that you intend to use so that it is easy to trace its location in your two tables.

j. Step 9 involves identifying the relevant prerequisite information (i.e., knowledge, skills, and content and practice standards) that students need to have in order successfully accomplish the goals of the unit. For this particular unit, identify the relevant prior information.

k. Step 10 involves planning for effective time management. This pertains to the last column in Table 12.4. Do not underestimate this aspect of the CPUP. Beginning teachers usually have trouble estimating the appropriate amount of time that students will need to learn each lesson in a unit. You need to remind yourself that your students are learning formal mathematical concepts and processes for the first time, so be reasonable. You also need to allot time for everyday or ongoing formative assessments, weekly and unit summative assessments, and, if necessary, reteaching sessions. Provide a breakdown and total number of 55-minute classroom sessions that you will need to achieve the goals and objectives of your unit.

l. Step 11 involves identifying relevant materials and resources that you will need in order to implement your activities effectively. Technology resources pertain to hardware (e.g., document camera) and software tools (e.g., apps). Printed resources and materials include worksheets, textbooks, and other visual tools for learning. Supplies pertain to typical school-related learning aids and tools, accessories, and manipulatives. Internet resources are links that are relevant to teaching and learning a unit. For this particular unit, identify the supplies, resources, and materials that matter.

m. Step 12 involves articulating accommodation-related issues and resources. This last component in CPUP addresses additional issues that pertain to the specific needs of your class. For example, if you have English learners and/or students with mathematical difficulties, you may want to discuss explicit strategies that you intend to use to help them succeed in learning the unit goal and lesson objectives. For this particular unit, identify accommodation strategies that you can use to help English learners and students with mathematical difficulties learn to subtract two-digit numbers proficiently before, during, and after each lesson.

12.6 CONTENT-PRACTICE LESSON PLANNING

Content-practice lesson planning involves developing, managing, and assessing an essential question in a detailed manner. You may construct lesson plans either daily, weekly, or based on the nature and complexity of a target content-practice learning objective. All exemplary content-practice lesson plans are clear, systematic, logical, and sufficiently thorough, meaning to say that any interested stakeholder, and especially substitutes, can easily imagine how your lessons are expected to unfold by simply reading the plans. Do remember that while lesson plans operate like scripts, they are not supposed to be read directly in class. Well-conceptualized lesson plans are also meant to help you anticipate or hypothesize emerging content-practice structures. Overall, good lesson plans help you teach in a coherent manner and provide a conducive and optimal environment for student and classroom learning. Certainly, James Scrivener's following point is worth noting: "In class, you teach the learners and not the plan." Do the following tasks below.

    a. Access the following links below to learn more about effective lesson planning.

https://docs.google.com/a/sjsu.edu/document/d/17H0IYY0ICX4PUtdp RGJXal_jemRhf2PIqpVK2U9TdcU/edit

http://www.crlt.umich.edu/gsis/p2_5

http://www.scholastic.com/teachers/article/new-teachers-guide-creating-lesson-plans

http://www.cal.org/caela/tools/program_development/elltoolkit/Part2-29LessonPlanning.pdf

    b. Use what you learned from the above links to construct a 55-minute content-practice lesson plan based on the CPUP you developed in the preceding section. Use the template shown in Table 12.7 to help you organize your lesson plan. Consider the following additional comments and instructions in relation to Table 12.7.

Under the *CCSSM Content Standard* row, this is a simple cut-and-paste from the CCSSM document. Identify the appropriate domain, cluster, and content standard/s that apply to your lesson. There is no need to paraphrase. Further, under *Standard*, if a content standard contains two or more related smaller standards, highlight in either **bold** or <u>underline</u> form the specific line (or lines) that applies (apply) to your lesson.

Under the *CCSSM Practice Standard/s* row, this is also a simple cut-and-paste from the CCSSM document. Refer to your Table 2.3 for specific primary practice action/s that you want your students to employ in learning the content standard you identified in the preceding section row. Do not be too eager to identify all practice standards that apply. Since you only have 55 minutes to teach your lesson, choose your practice action(s) wisely. Fill in the secondary cluster and related practice standard/s, if necessary.

Under the *Prerequisite CCSSM Content Standard/s* row, this is also a simple cut-and-paste from the CCSSM document. Identify the prerequisite content standard/s that students need to know to learn the new lesson well. You may need to highlight in either **bold** or <u>underline</u> form the appropriate line/s from the content standard/s describing the prerequisite knowledge.

Under the *Essential Math Question* row, this is a simple cut-and-paste from your unit plan.

Under the *CR Objective/s* row, the acronym SWBAT stands for "Students Would Be Able To." There are two things that you need to consider in writing your lesson objective(s). First, the relevant CCSSM objective may already provide you with the appropriate language in which case you simply cut and paste. Second, you may use the Cognitive Rigor Matrix to help you decide whether you need to construct a more specific and measurable objective or set of objectives than the one provided in the CCSSM document. In either case, analyze the learning objective according to the matrix and record your result by coding in the following manner: [DOK #, TOT], where DOK # refers to the level of depth of knowledge and TOT pertains to the target type of thinking. Remember that each CR Objective is a learning outcome that will be assessed in a formative or summative context. Also, be realistic about the number of objectives that you intend to assess in a 55-minute lesson.

Under the *Target SB Summative Assessment Tasks (Claim/s & Item/s)* row, while you are not expected to implement a summative assessment task at the end of a 55-minute lesson, being aware of such tasks can inform the manner in which you develop appropriate formative tasks. In fact, any summative assessment task can be used in a formative context with some modification. Try to obtain released summative assessment tasks that match your content-practice standards and CR objectives. Also, identify the appropriate claim and item number that apply to each task. Refer to item (v) in section 10.5 to help you recall how this task assignment processing is accomplished.

Under the *Supporting Material/s and Resource/s* row, draw on your unit plan and identify relevant technological tools, printed matter, supplies, and, if applicable, internet resources that you intend to use to accomplish your lesson objective.

Under the *Lesson Activity* row, you need to address the following key events in your 55-minute lesson: beginning event; during event; and ending event. Consider the following two steps: First, determine the teaching model/s that you intend to use to teach your lesson. For illustration purposes, assume the C-R-A and SDAIE teaching models, with levels of collaborative learning actions (i.e.: work independently, work together in small groups, and work together as a class) providing additional teaching/ learning support. Second, describe under *Event Sequence* how each phase in the C-R-A, particular SDAIE strategies, and each level of collaborative learning action will be implemented in your lesson. Also include under each phase your planned activities and labeled formative assessment tasks that will be used to support teaching and learning in that phase. Provide explicit practice-driven guide questions and target responses to help you gain a sense of how your lesson activity will evolve. See to it that your guide questions are aligned with your practice standard objective/s. Budget your time wisely so that you are able to accomplish every part of your lesson activity within the allotted time and in a reasonable manner.

Under the *Formative Assessment Task (Claim/s & Item/s)* row, provide details and analyses of all labeled formative assessment tasks that you identified in your Lesson Activity section. See to it that every task has a claim number. Remember that all tasks, stipulated CCSSM content and practice standards, and CR learning objectives must align well together.

Under the *Additional Notes* row, identify important issues, concerns, reminders, and other details that you think are pertinent to know regarding your lesson. For example, if your lesson will employ a SDAIE strategy, you may want to state your target academic language objective(s) that you want your students to achieve in addition to the CCSSM content-practice standard objectives. A second example involves differentiated instruction. If your lesson will have a differentiated component, you may want to provide details regarding steps that you need to consider in order to successfully implement it in class. A third example involves issues relevant to conducting collaborative learning. You simply do not ask students to work together in pairs or in groups, which means you may want to provide steps and indicators that will help you implement an effective group work actvity. Refer to sections 13.3 and 13.4 for details regarding how to set up, implement, and process collaborative learning in the math classroom. A fourth example involves using concrete or technology-based tools. You may want to provide details relevant to their implementation before, during, and/or after instruction.

12.7 A PLANNING PROJECT

In this section, you will develop your own CPUP, lesson plans, and assessments based on certain requirements. Do the following tasks below.

a. Choose a chapter in any K-5 mathematics textbook that has at least five individual lessons or sections.
b. Develop a CPUP for the chapter. Use the template shown in Tables 12.3 through 12.6 to help you organize your CPUP.
c. Develop a lesson plan with the following specifications: (1) one lesson employs both C-R-A and SDAIE; (2) another lesson combines C-R-A and cultural responsiveness; (3) a third lesson is intended for a flipped class. Use Table 12.7 for guidance. See to it that all assessment tasks are presented and analyzed appropriately.
d. Develop a project as an alternative form of summative assessment for the unit. Refer to section 10.6 for details regarding essential project components and scoring rubrics and guidelines.

167

Table 12.3. Content-practice unit plan template

Subject and Grade Level	
Unit Title	
Unit Content Big Idea(s) and Essential Questions	
Big Idea Statement	
Key Concepts and/or Processes	
Essential Question for Each Section in the Unit	
Unit Content Overview	
Unit Content Trajectory in the Form of a Concept Map	
Rough Drafts of Lessons	
See Table 12.4	
Unit Formative Summative Assessment Plan, Details, and Analysis	
See Tables 12.5 and 12.6 for the analysis	
Prerequisite Knowledge to the Unit	
Breakdown and Total Number of 55-Minute Classroom Sessions Needed to Achieve Unit Goals and Lesson Objectives	
Unit Materials and Resources	
Technology Resources	
Printed Resources and Materials	
Supplies	
Internet Resources	
Accommodation Issues and Resources	

Table 12.4. Lesson plan sequence template draft

Essential Question	Content Standard	Practice Standards	Lesson Overview	Appropriate Activities and Relevant Materials and Resources	Formative and Summative Assessment Tasks	Number of 55-Min Sessions

Table 12.5. Formative and summative content-practice assessment mapping

Content-Practice-Assessment Analysis		Formative Assessment Tasks						Summative Assessment Tasks					
		E.g., Labeled Task 1									E.g., Labeled Task 3		
CCSSM Domains	Counting and Cardinality												
	Operations and Algebraic Thinking												
	Whole Numbers and Operations in Base 10												
	Fractions and Operations												
	Measurement and Data												
	Geometry												
CCSSM Practices	Make sense of problems and persevere in solving them												
	Reason abstractly and quantitatively												
	Construct viable arguments and critique the reasoning of others												
	Model with mathematics												
	Use appropriate tools strategically												
	Attend to precision												
	Look for and make use of structure												
	Look for and express regularity in repeated reasoning												

Table 12.6. Task Analysis template by depth and type of thinking

Depth of Thinking + Type of Thinking	Level 1 Recall and Reproduction	Level 2 Basic Skill and Concepts	Level 3 Strategic Thinking and Reasoning	Level 4 Extended Thinking
Remember				
Understand		E.g., labeled formative task 1		
Apply				
Analyze				
Evaluate				E.g., labeled summative task 1
Create				

Table 12.7. Content-practice lesson plan template

		Date	Teacher	Subject & Grade Level
CCSSM Content Standard	Domain			
	Cluster			
	Standard			
CCSSM Practice Standard/s	Primary Cluster			
	Specific Action/s			
	Secondary Cluster, if applicable			
	Specific Action/s			
Prerequisite CCSSM Content Standard/s				
Essential Math Question				
CR Objective/sw		At the end of the 55-minute lesson, SWBAT		
Target SB Summative Assessment (Claim/s & Item/s)				

Supporting Material/s and Resource/s				
Lesson Activity	**Allotted Time**	**Event Sequence**	**Guide Question/s**	**Target Response/s**
		Beginning		
		During		
		Closing		
Formative Assessment (Claim/s & Item/s)				
Additional Notes				

ORCHESTRATING A CONTENT-PRACTICE DRIVEN MATH CLASSROOM

In this chapter, you will deal with issues relevant to setting up and running effective content-practice driven mathematics classrooms. Such classrooms typically provide a positive climate that supports meaningful engagement with the content and practice standards. Having such a climate also enables you to teach in ways that help your students develop a strong mathematical disposition and see intellectual struggle as an integral aspect of learning mathematical concepts, skills, and applications. The first four sections in this chapter address issues relevant to persistence and struggle, including ways that you can support them to perform consistently in such intense moments in both individual and collaborative contexts.

From a practical standpoint, all stakeholders want effective math classrooms taking place at all times. They want you and your students to succeed together. When your math class is effective, everybody is, in fact, happy beginning with you and your students and then your colleagues in the same building and in adjacent rooms, your math coach, your principal, your superintendent, and the parents of your students. Setting up an effective math classroom will require a strong management plan that is capable of providing optimal learning for all students, eliminating or minimizing disruptions, and dealing with potential behavior problems. The last three sections in this chapter address such issues, which should help you conceptualize meaningful and appropriate preventive and supportive strategies as your students learn different aspects of classroom life and work requirements. However, it is wise to remember that your model colleagues (e.g.: math coach and seasoned and award-winning veteran teachers) can also provide you with additional and necessary contextual information and advice.

13.1 PERSISTENCE AND STRUGGLES IN MATH CLASSROOMS

Access the following link below, which compares Eastern and Western perspectives on the nature of intelligence and struggle. Answer the questions that follow.

http://www.npr.org/blogs/health/2012/11/12/164793058/struggle-for-smarts-how-eastern-and-western-cultures-tackle-learning

a. How are notions of "struggle" and "academic excellence" perceived in Eastern and Western contexts?
b. What do you learn from studies that compare differing cultural practices on intelligence and struggle?

Access the following article below, which discusses ways in which learning and learning environments can be designed to effectively support cognitive growth and mathematical disposition among students. Answer the questions that follow.

De Corte, Erik. (1995). Fostering cognitive growth: A perspective from research on mathematics learning and instruction. *Educational Psychologist*, 30(1), 37-46.

c. Describe a few characteristics of effective learning processes. Develop possible implications for mathematics teaching and learning.
d. Learn the five design principles for powerful learning environments and develop implications for your own practice.
e. What is Realistic Mathematics Education (RME)? What can you learn from RME about meaningful and effective mathematics teaching, learning, and management?

Access the following articles below, which tackle the issue of lack of engagement in school mathematics in different contexts. As you read the articles, focus on the implications of the authors' findings in your developing classroom management practice. Answer the questions that follow.

Sullivan, Peter, Tobias, Steve, and McDonough, Andrea. (2006). Perhaps the decision of some students not to engage in learning mathematics in schools is deliberate. *Educational Studies in Mathematics, 62,* 81-99.

Singh, Kusum, Granville, Monique, and Dika, Sandra. (2002). Mathematics and science achievement: Effects of motivation, interest, and academic engagement. *Journal of Educational Research,* 95(6), 323-332.

f. What are some possible sources of students' (lack of) perseverance as they relate to engagement in mathematics?
g. How might you set up your classroom in ways that could effectively eliminate students' underparticipation and underachievement in mathematics?

13.2 FOSTERING PERSISTENT CONTENT-PRACTICE LEARNERS

Engaging elementary students to pursue tasks that are aligned with the CCSSM means engaging them in problem solving activity. In section 2.4, you learned four different problem-solving contexts that relate to the context-practice learning of mathematics. Reread that section before you engage in the following tasks below.

Access the following link below, which discusses strategies for helping students develop persistence in flexible problem solving contexts. Answer the questions that follow.

http://mason.gmu.edu/~jsuh4/Persistent%20Flexible%20Problem%20 Solvers2008.pdf

a. Discuss target characteristics that will help all students become good problem solvers in mathematics.

b. Slide 26 shows a universal design for learning framework (UDL) for mathematics instruction. According the Higher Education Opportunity Act, a UDL is "a scientifically valid framework for guiding educational practice that (a) provides flexibility in the ways information is presented, in the ways students respond or demonstrate knowledge and skills, and in the ways students are engaged; and (b) reduces barriers in instruction, provides appropriate accommodations, supports, and challenges, and maintains high achievement expectations for all students, including students with disabilities and students who are limited English proficient."

How might you design content-practice mathematical tasks that could promote flexible problem solving?

c. What information do you gain from the reflections provided by teachers Brooke and Gwen when they restructured their classrooms around problem solving?

Access the following link below, which talks about the different aspects of mathematical activity in a social context.

http://www.tlu.ee/~kpata/haridustehnoloogiaTLU/constructivsit.pdf

d. What is the *emergent perspective* on learning mathematics in a classroom context?

e. What are social norms? How are they distinguished from sociomathematical norms? How do both types of norms contribute to the emergence of classroom mathematical practices?

f. Table 13.1 shows a classroom manifesto based on the authors' emergent perspective. Describe possible students' experiences in mathematics classrooms that abide by the manifesto.

13.3 DEVELOPING EFFECTIVE COLLABORATIVE CONTENT-PRACTICE LEARNING THROUGH COMPLEX INSTRUCTION

Complex Instruction (CI) emerged from the work of Elizabeth Cohen and her Stanford education colleagues who were concerned about providing meaningful and equitable collaborative learning experiences for all students in everyday classrooms. CI takes a much more structured approach to collaborative learning than simply having students work in pairs or in groups. In CI, there are very clear group work and group task requirements that need to be accomplished. Certainly, it is easy to plan classroom work by having all students work in pairs or in groups. However, the most difficult problem is how to make group learning work effectively for all members in every team from start to finish.

A LEARNING MANIFESTO

Social Norms

1. I will allways explain my solution or way of thinking, that is, why I think it makes sense to me.

2. It is okay to generate a different solution or explanation to a problem.

3. It is okay to ask if a different solution or explanation is possible to better understand a problem.
   - It is okay to ask if somebody else can solve the problem in a different way.
   - It is okay if somebody did something differently to solve the problem.

4. I will do my best to make sense of somebody else's solution. I need to be respectful.

5. It is okay to ask clarifying questions if I don't understand an explanation or solution.

6. In a situation of conflict, I should be courteous and ask a clarifying question.

7. I should say if I don't understand and that I need more explanation.

Sociomathematical Norms

8. What counts as an acceptable solution or explanation will always be discussed and negotiated by all.
   - I can use my process to solve a problem, but I should be able to explain it and why it works.

9. When a classmate presents a different solution or explanation, the following process will be followed:
   - Be ready to explain why the solution or explanation makes sense.
   - All of us will assess whether the solution or explanation makes sense.

10. I understand that my solution to a problem may not be the best.
    - Somebody may have a more sophisticated or efficient way of solving the problem and I should know why.

Figure 13.1 A learning manifesto

CI assumes the following three conditions below.

- There is a diverse curriculum that enables all students with different abilities to experience success in developing higher-order thinking skills through purposeful group work activities.
- Instruction focuses on training students to work effectively in groups through activities that employ and develop cooperative norms and explicit team role playing.
- There is value in equitable learning that deals with treat status issues proactively through activities and reflection that encourage all learners, especially the underperforming ones, to participate equally in discussions and value their contributions to group work.

CI tasks should be groupworthy, multiple ability-based, and sufficiently open-ended so that all students are encouraged to work together and contribute to the discussion. Think about groupworthy tasks in terms of the UDL framework noted in the preceding section (i.e., item 13.2 (b)). When you implement CI, your task as the classroom teacher involves observing groups, providing timely feedback, and dealing with treat status issues. Feedback can take many forms, of course, but you need to see to it that all team members are performing their assigned roles in a respectful manner. Work with a team of four students and do the following tasks below.

a. Access the following links below, which provide details relevant to designing classroom instruction in mathematics around CI.

http://math.arizona.edu/~cemela/english/content/workingpapers/2010NCTM RossTsinnajinnieCivil04_24.pdf

http://nrich.maths.org/content/id/7011/nrich%20paper.pdf

http://complexinstruction5.wikispaces.com/

Identify teaching practices that support the use of CI in classroom activity. What other issues are not addressed in CI?

b. One complicated issue among elementary school students involves helping them learn to deal with their emotions. Since CI capitalizes on meaningful and supportive interactions among members in a team, students may need some explicit instruction in terms of how to process their emotions in group activity. Access the following article below, which addresses the issue of whether and how emotional intelligence can be taught to children.

http://www.nytimes.com/2013/09/15/magazine/can-emotional-intelligence-be-taught.html?_r=0

What is social-emotional learning (SEL)? How can teachers use SEL strategies to support CI-based learning?

c. Given what you know about CI and SEL, discuss ways in which both strategies can assist in facilitating elementary students' content-practice learning of the CCSSM.

13.4 OTHER COLLABORATIVE CONTENT-PRACTICE LEARNING TECHNIQUES

Access the file "classactivities" from the link below, which describes nine strategies that encourage students to work cooperatively in groups. Work with a group of three students and answer the questions that follow.

http://complexinstruction5.wikispaces.com/

a. Which cooperative learning strategies are doable in the math classroom? Which ones might be difficult to implement, and why?

b. Do you need to implement all the cooperative learning strategies you learned in this section during your first year of teaching? Explain.

c. How might you prepare yourself to teach in a collaborative context that supports content-practice learning of mathematics?

d. What do you need to do before and after students work in groups and during the time they are working in groups?

13.5 DEVELOPING AN OPTIMAL CONTENT-PRACTICE LEARNING ENVIRONMENT FOR ALL ELEMENTARY STUDENTS

Work with a pair and do the following tasks below.

a. The *What Works Clearinghouse in Education* (WWC) link below provides evidence-based information around effective classroom instruction in mathematics.

http://ies.ed.gov/ncee/wwc/default.aspx

Search "Back to School Tips" in the WWC for: (1) recommendations regarding how to help students deal with mathematical problem solving; and (2) evidence of effective math interventions in schools and districts.

b. Access the following two links below, which provide information regarding how to effectively organize instruction and study time and plan effective interventions for elementary students.

http://ies.ed.gov/ncee/wwc/pdf/practice_guides/20072004.pdf
http://ies.ed.gov/ncser/pubs/20133001/pdf/20133001.pdf

What kinds of classroom environment and instructional practices support successful learning among children? What educational practices can help improve the manner in which they learn mathematics?

c. Access the following two links below, which provide information about best instructional practices, in particular, Response-to-Intervention (RtI) strategies, for students with mathematical difficulties.

http://nichcy.org/wp-content/uploads/docs/eemath.pdf

http://ies.ed.gov/ncee/wwc/pdf/practice_guides/rti_math_pg_042109.pdf

http://educationnorthwest.org/resource/1679

What is RtI applied to mathematics? What does RtI recommend insofar as instruction in mathematics and the use of intervention materials are concerned?

d. Access the link below, which provides instructional recommendations for teaching fractions.

http://www.edvanceresearch.com/images/fractions_pg_093010.pdf

How well do the general recommendations for effective instruction noted in the preceding items align with the specific recommendations for fraction learning at the elementary level?

e. Access the following link below, which provides instructional recommendations for supporting females in elementary classrooms.

http://ies.ed.gov/ncee/wwc/pdf/practice_guides/20072003.pdf

How can instruction be used to help young females strengthen their beliefs about their ability to do mathematics? What strategies can promote their interests toward the subject and encourage them to pursue a career path in mathematics? What activities can help them further strengthen their spatial skills that are pertinent to successful mathematical learning and understanding? You already know something about SDAIE-driven teaching in section 12.2.4.

f. Access the follow links below and identify additional instructional strategies that can help English learners obtain cognitive academic language proficiency in mathematics.

http://schools.nyc.gov/NR/rdonlyres/9E62A2F2-4C5C-4534-968B-5487A7BD3742/0/GeneralMathStrategiesforELLs_082811.pdf

https://uteach.utexas.edu/sites/default/files/files/SixKeyStrategiesELL.pdf

http://www.tsusmell.org/downloads/Conferences/2005/Moore-Harris_2005.pdf

https://www.mheonline.com/glencoemath/pdf/ell.pdf

13.6 DEALING WITH POTENTIAL BEHAVIOR PROBLEMS

In this section you will learn general classroom management strategies (CMS). CMS should be implemented proactively so that all students understand that they are meant to help them learn mathematics in a safe environment. When you implement CMS in your own classroom, you need to consider at least two issues. The first issue deals with the fact that your personality, confidence, and knowledge of students' cultures influence the manner in which you implement CMS. While the internet will provide you with good, professional, and legal CMS for just about any kind of behavior problem, your personal, social, cultural, and other environmental constraints will ultimately shape your CMS. Some teachers, though, share the view that you need to develop a professional mindset about CMS. The second issue that should concern you deals with the fact that there is no any one-size-fits-all CMS that will work effectively for all students. However, that fact should not discourage you from learning about successful stories of CMS. Do the following tasks below.

a. Access the following resources below and answer the question that follow.

Englehart, Joshua. (2012). Five half-truths about classroom management. *The Clearing House*, 85, 70-73.

http://www.calstatela.edu/faculty/jshindl/cm/Ten%20Biggest%20 Mistakes%20Made%20by%20Teachers%209-04b.htm

Identify at least ten ideas that will help guide your emerging CMS.

b. Central to effectively implementing CMS in your classroom involves the need to frontload as soon as possible. For example, some teachers employ the 3F frontloading practice, which involves having students practice routines and other classroom rules on the first of day, the first week, and the first month of the school year. CMS that are practiced in class are intended to be preventive. Access the following link below and develop a list of top ten specific actions that you want your students to accomplish by the end of the: (1) first day; (2) first week; and (3) first month of the school year.

https://www.msu.edu/~dunbarc/dunbar3.pdf

c. Classroom CMS require a firm understanding of school and district rules and policies regarding attendance, suspension, time off, and so on. Search the internet for two to three samples of such rules and policies. Discuss similarities, differences, and essential components.

d. Access the following link below, which discusses three types of discipline that characterize various aspects of CMS.

http://ci.columbia.edu/ci/tools/0511/

Assess the following teachers' responses below in relation to the stated classroom incidents.

(i) When an incident occurs, small or big, I quickly react to it by implementing a corrective strategy. They need to show me the appropriate behavior all the time.

(ii) I like to confront disruptive action with an offensive reaction. That way my students know that I am in charge.

(iii) I cannot help but hold a grudge against a student who misbehaves in my class. I tend not to move on until the student knows what proper behavior means.

(iv) When an incident happens, I reinforce my expectations quickly rather than enforce a corrective rule mixed with some kind of punishment.

(v) My students were so distracted by the manipulatives we used in class today. As a consequence, I told them that we will never use manipulatives ever again. They are not ready.

(vi) Today my first-period class entered my room in a disorganized manner. A few of them came in late after the bell. When they sat down, they refused to listen and simply started talking to each other. Since they were not interested in learning and being respectful, I decided to give them free time. I hope they realize how much of their own time is wasted whenever they feel like behaving like that in my class. I will not teach a class that does not know how to behave in a respectful manner.

e. Access the following link below, which provides research-based recommendations for reducing common behavior problems among students. Compare the CMS you generated in (a) and (b) with the recommendations noted in the document.

http://ies.ed.gov/ncee/wwc/pdf/practice_guides/behavior_pg_092308.pdf

13.7 ASSIGNING HOMEWORK, GRADING AND TESTING, AND SEATING

Should elementary students do homework, where homework means tasks that students accomplish during nonschool hours? What are some benefits of having students do homework problems or tasks? Are there compelling reasons that can tell us that doing homework is not helpful to children's learning and (academic) development in the long term? These perennial issues about the benefits and disadvantages of assigning homework are still not settled because there is no solid and converging research evidence that indicates strong correlational and causal relationships between student achievement and doing homework. But it is important to be aware of the issues and be open-minded enough to consider the pros and cons of assigning homework, especially when young children are involved. Do the following tasks below with a group.

a. Search the internet for at least three to five articles that discuss the benefits and disadvantages of assigning homework. Identify the claims under each perspective and develop either your own or your group's perspective on the matter.

b. Access the following links below, which provide homework tips from the National Council of Teachers of Mathematics (NCTM).

http://www.nctm.org/resources/content.aspx?id=6338
http://www.nctm.org/news/content.aspx?id=13816

Suppose you intend to incorporate homework in your teaching practices. Generate possible homework rules and strategies for processing homework in class.

c. How might you assign homework tasks in ways that will support growth in students' content-practice learning of mathematics. What potential issues do you anticipate parents or responsible caretakers might have on homework tasks that are designed around the content-practice standards? How might you address such issues so that parents and caretakers know that such tasks are intended to help their children and wards succeed in mathematics, progress through middle school, and prepare them for future workplace and 21st century skills?

Grading is an important aspect of a teacher's job. Unlike homework, grading these days is linked to local, state, and federal accountability structures that schools and districts carefully develop, implement, and monitor. Do the following tasks below.

d. Search the internet to learn about *Adequate Yearly Progress* (AYP) and *Academic Performance Index* (API). What are AYP and API all about? How are schools and districts affected by AYP and API scores?

e. Search the internet to learn about *benchmark assessments* (BAs) in mathematics. What are BAs and how do schools and districts develop them and use the results to inform classroom instruction?

f. Access the following link below, which provides a list of recommendations for using student achievement data to support instructional decision making.

http://ies.ed.gov/ncee/wwc/pdf/practice_guides/dddm_pg_092909.pdf

Carefully read each recommendation and assess its significance and value in terms of how and what you teach in your own classroom.

g. Access the following links below, which provides grading tips from the NCTM.

http://www.nctm.org/resources/content.aspx?id=6336

Which suggestions are familiar to you, and which ones are new? Share other tips that you might want to add to the list.

h. Inservice elementary teachers usually discuss grading schemes either in grade-level teams or at the school level with principals and colleagues across departments. In some school districts, such schemes are implemented as a district policy. Search the internet for at least three grading schemes in mathematics at the elementary level. How are they similar and different? Which components appear to be essential?

i. Many teachers share the view that if students are prepared really well to take a test, then half the battle is won. Do you agree?
Access the following link below, which provides test preparation tips from the NCTM.

http://www.nctm.org/resources/content.aspx?id=2147483737

Which suggestions do you share, and which ones do you find troubling? Share other tips that you might want to add to the list.

j. Access the following link below, which introduces you to issues surrounding high stakes testing (HST).

http://www.nctm.org/uploadedFiles/Lessons_and_Resources/dialogues/May-June_1998/1998-05.pdf

What is HST? Why do you need to be concerned about it? Reflect on the various responses on HST in the document and develop your own response to the question of whether HST should drive mathematics curriculum and instruction.

Assigning elementary students to their seats in the classroom is one very important aspect of classroom management. Optimal learning, especially in mathematics classrooms, depends on how well you are able to arrange individual students in your class(es) so that disruptions are minimized or preferably eliminated. Work with a team and do the following task below.

k. Search the internet for effective classroom seating arrangement tips and rules. Explain how each tip or rule matters to learning.
l. Search the internet for seating arrangement tips for elementary students: (i) with behavior problems; (ii) with attention deficit hyperactivity disorder; and (iii) that require English language assistance.

13.8 A CLASSROOM MANAGEMENT PLAN PROJECT

Use the structure from the link below to help you develop a classroom management plan (CMP). See to it that you address all five components in your CMP in sufficient detail by drawing on your learnings from the preceding chapters on teaching, learning, and assessment and the sections in this chapter.

http://people.umass.edu/~afeldman/beingnewteacher/classmanageplan.html

The following sites below provide well-conceived samples that can inform your own CMP.

http://www.calstatela.edu/faculty/jshindl/cm/Example%20CMPs.htm
http://sarahsmalley.wordpress.com/244-2/
http://web.utk.edu/~rmcneele/classroom/management.html
http://users.manchester.edu/Student/JLCollins/ProfWeb2/
CM--Classroom%20Management%20Plan.pdf
http://caje33.wikispaces.com/file/view/BSM_ManagementHandout4.pdf

CPSIA information can be obtained
at www.ICGtesting.com
Printed in the USA
FSOW02n1934310516
21021FS